The Divided States of United Lies!

(The so-called "United States of North America," in Disguise!)

By
The Worldwide People's Revolution!®

Book 058

(A Photo of a Map of the United States)

Copyright Dedication and Introduction

By Dr. Samuel Walker Edison, Ph.D., MA, BS, and QC.

ISBN-13: 978-1536-8169-52
ISBN-10: 1536-8169-57

00-01 [_] This Inspired Book is COPYRIGHTED 2016—2020 AD, by **The Worldwide People's Revolution!®** All Rights are Reserved by the Federal Burden of Investigation (FBI), the Central Unintelligent Agencies (CIA), the Federal Emergency Mismanagement Agency (FEMA), the Immigration and Neutralization Service (INS), the Bad Foods and Good Drugs Administration (FDA), the Bureau of Alcoholics, Tobacco, and Firearms Fanatics with Explosives (BATF), and many other Phony Federal DEPARTments and Agencies, which **"The New RIGHTEOUS One-World Goverment"** will have no Use for: beCause each Beautiful Planned City State will Govern itself, according to its own Elected Laws and Flexible Rules, after all of the Like-minded People have been SEPARATED from one another by Filling Out and Filing **"The Complete SURVEYS of our VALUES!" (SURVEYS of Religious Spiritual Political Governmental Sexual Social Moral Economic Business Labor Habitual and Miscellaneous VALUES!)**, whereby the People who are like Sheeps and Goats can be SEPARATED from the People who are like Lions and Wolves: beCause it is not Right to Tax Good Honest Hardworking People, just to Support Lazy and Crazy People, like Politicans, who want to Live off of the Labors of other People, who are not even Needed for True Prosperity. †§‡

00-02 [_] No Portion of this Inspired Book shall be Reproduced by any Means for Sale without Written Permission from **The Worldwide People's Revolution!®** However, with that Permission, anyone is the World may Reproduce Exact Copies for Sale, and KEEP 90 percent (90%) of the Net Profits for their own Personal Prosperity: beCause **The Worldwide People's Revolution!®** only wants 10% of the Net Profits for the Construction of **"The Great World TEMPLE of PEACE,"** in Jerusalem, which will be the Tallest and Largest Building in the World, being nearly a Mile Tall and 8+ Miles in Diameter, being Built in 60 Great Stone Terraces, having 10 Smaller Terraces within each Great Terrace, which will have Beautiful Stone Dome Home Complexes within those Smaller Terraces, where the Elected Officials of **"The New RIGHTEOUS One-World Government"** will take up Housekeeping, along with their Voluntary Servants, which Officials will be Paid the same Wages as Dishwashers and Gardeners, according to **"A List of FAIR Swanky Wages,"** whereby Justice will be Served. In other Words, those Elected Officials will put in their 8 Hours per Day, and Live and Work in the Great Temple, having all of their Necessities Supplied by **"The Swanky Associations of Working Soldiers!" (A Fascinating Collection of Various Kinds of Voluntary Working Soldiers!)** By The Worldwide People's Revolution!® Book 018.

00-03 [_] This Inspired Book is now DEDICATED to the Permanently Retired and Dismembered Members of the Federal Government of **The Divided States of United Lies!** Yes, they may now Stop Dialing for Dollars, and go to Work in their own Luscious All-Mineral

(The so-called "United States of North America," in Disguise!)

Organic Gardens and Home-craft Workshops and Sales Shops within those **"GLORIOUS Swanky Hotels Castles and Fortress!" (Beautiful Planned City States for WISE Intelligent Well-Educated People with Common Sense and Good Understanding!) By The Worldwide People's Revolution!®** Book 019.

00-04 [_] O Doctor Samuel Walker Edison, are you SERIOUS? Does **The Worldwide People's Revolution!®** have Intentions of Retiring almost all Politicians, Worldwide?

00-05 [_] Yes, you are Understanding it Correctly at the Core of it: beCause, we, the Masses of People in this World of Woes, have had Enough of their Lies and False Promises. Therefore, they will all be "Put Out to Pasture," as the Old Saying goes: beCause we Tax Slaves, Interest Slaves, Insurance Slaves, Drug Slaves, Sex Slaves, and Work Slaves have had Enough of their Nonsense. In Fact, we Refuse to Vote for another Politician, until he or she has Filled Out and Filed **"The Complete SURVEYS of our VALUES!" (SURVEYS of Religious Spiritual Political Governmental Sexual Social Moral Economic Business Labor Habitual and Miscellaneous VALUES!)**, whereby we Electors might Learn whatever they Sincerely Believe: beCause of Checking the Appropriate Boxes that they Agree with. For Example, if they Check this Box: [_] I Promise to tell the Truth — and then they get Caught telling Lies, they will Lose their Jobs: beCause it is Possible and most Practical for all Leaders to be Perfectly Honest at all Times, once we get **"The New RIGHTEOUS One-World Government"** Established, and without going to War, which is WHY the Subtitle of that Inspired Book is called: **"HOW to Establish a Righteous One-World Government without Going to WAR!"** Book 056.

00-06 [_] O Doctor Sam, will that Good Government not have any Top Secrets to KEEP? For Example, will it not have any Secret Weapons in its Arsenal of Weapons, whereby it can Defeat any Enemies?

00-07 [_] NO, it will not have any Enemies: beCause they will all be Defeated by **"The Swanky Sword of Divine Truths!"** — which is otherwise known as: **"The Sharp Sword of Divine Truths!" (The Most Powerful Weapon in the Whole Universe!) By The Worldwide People's Revolution!®** Book 067. Yes, it will be used Wisely by our Elected King, who will Remove the Head of Lies with one Swift Stroke, you might say, at: **"The Great Worldwide TELEVISED Court HEARING!" (That Great Meeting of the Most Intelligent Minds!) By The Worldwide People's Revolution!®** Book 041.

00-08 [_] So, O Doctor Sam, just Exactly WHO is your Elected King?

00-09 [_] Well, he is the Person who has the most Reasonable Solutions for our Massive Problems, who could be just about any Man on the Earth, who has Filled Out and Filed **"The Complete SURVEYS of our VALUES!"** Book 059.

00-10 [_] So, O Doctor Samuel Walker Edison, it Sounds as if **The Worldwide People's Revolution!®** has it all figured out. Therefore, how Long will it be before **The Worldwide People's Revolution!®** takes Over the Whole World? {See www.Amazon.com for: **"Justifications for Capitalizations!" (WHY The Worldwide People's Revolution!® Defies the School of Fools by Capitalizing Love and Hate!)** Book 049.}

The Fascinating Menu for a Feast of Provable Truths!

Chapter 01 — Just how DIVIDED are the Divided States of United Lies? ... page 5

Chapter 02 — Why are the Eyeballs of Uncle Sam Crossed? ... 11

Chapter 03 — WHY God has not Revealed himself to Humanity! ... 13

Chapter 04 — *"Many are Called; but, Few are Chosen!"* ... 14

Chapter 05 — The Insanity of Election Deceptions! ... 16

Chapter 06 — Just how RIGHTEOUS are the Masses of People? ... 19

Chapter 07 — Loaning Money for Interest ... 24

Chapter 08 — Segregation has now become a GOOD Thing! ... 26

Chapter 09 — Equal Opportunities must be Guaranteed! ... 30

Chapter 10 — The Tough Questions ... 32

Chapter 11 — Gun Control without Guns! ... 34

Chapter 12 — A Sure Cure for Sins! ... 36

Chapter 13 — Happy Black People ... 38

Chapter 14 — The Birth of a New Nation! ... 41

Chapter 15 — The Conclusion ... 43

Chapter 16 — Other Fascinating Literature by the same Inspired Author ... 45

The Enticement is on the Back Cover ... page 52

(The so-called "United States of North America," in Disguise!)

— Chapter 01 —

Just how DIVIDED are the Divided States of United Lies?

01-01 [_] Well, other than being Divided into Various STATES, most of the People in the United States of America are Divided in many Ways. For Example, they have some 400+ Contradictory False Religions, with well over 200 False Translations of their *"Unholy Mutilated Bibles,"* as the Irreverent Snake calls them, whose Twisted Tale of Lies is a Mile Long, you might say; but, it is very Colorful and Fascinating, if you Study it Carefully: beCause it is mostly Comical Sarcasms.

01-02 [_] I am sorry to Inform you; but, even after Graduating from **"The Public School of IGNERUNT FQLZ,"** I do not know what a Sarcasm IS.

01-03 [_] Well, that is Understandable, seeing that most Children are not Taught very many Important Things in the Public School of Ignorant Fools, which has more than 20 Ways to Spell the single Sound of "OO," as in: "Sch**oo**l, r**u**le, d**o**, sh**oe**, thr**ough**, t**wo**, l**ieu**, cr**ew**, bl**ue**, fr**ui**t, man**eu**ver, S**iou**x, r**hu**barb, **rheu**matism, rendezv**ous**, gh**oul**, and p**ooh**" — etc., etc., etc. Yes, nearly every Sound in the English Language has 5 to 40 Different Ways to SPELL IT, which Causes Great Confusion within the Minds of Innocent Children, who would much Prefer to "Spel their Werdz in sum Kunsistunt Maner."

A-[_] I Agree — it would be much Better for everyone, if we should Spell all of our Words in some Consistent Manner.

B-[_] I Believe that it would Help us to Learn HOW to "reed and riit."

C-[_] I Confess that I am already Lost in the Darkness of Ignorance: because I have no Idea what you People are "Talking" about.

D-[_] Well, Dumbo, we are Talking about Spelling our Words in "FUNETIK Ingglish."

E-[_] I am already Educated, and do not Need any Phonetic English Lessons to "Masterbaat" my Mind on.

F-[_] I Fail to Understand WHY any Intelligent Well-Educated Person in this World of Wonders would not Gladly Accept the "Buutee uv Simplisitee" that is Employed in Swanky "Funetik Ingglish," whereby little Children could "Lern how tq reed and riit in just u Daa oor 2," and then spell any Word in the English Language on a Computer Keyboard, if they could Pronounce the "Werd" Correctly.

G-[_] God knows that THAT is the Major Problem: beCause they are not Able to Pronounce the Words CORE-rectly, at the Cores of them. For Example, some People say

"Nq Oorleenz," while others say, "Nq Oorlinz," or "Nq Oorleeunz." Therefore, the Children would become even more "Kunfuuzd" than ever with "Swangkless Funetik Ingglish." In other Words, in order to be of First Class Quality "Swanky" Phonetic English, there would have to be an Official "Funetik Ingglish Dikshuneiree," which would Naturally not be Accepted by large Groups of People. For Example, the People who Live in the Southern United States would not be Pronouncing their Words like the People in New England States, much less like the People in Western States, who all have Different ACCENTS.

H-[_] HUMBUG! The People in the South could Learn how to Speak like the People in the West, if they just Followed "Thu KEE TQ PROONUNSEEAASHUN," which can be found in: **"LIGHTNING Versus the Lightning Bug!" (HOW almost Everyone can become Moderately RICH, without Telling Any Lies nor Selling Any Trash!) By The Worldwide People's Revolution!® Book 001.**

I-[_] I am an Innocent Person, who Loves the Beauty of Simplicity. Therefore, if someone Wants to spell his or her Words in "Swangkee Funetik Ingglish," it is Okay with me: beCause I am Able to "Reed it and Riit it." However, it might not be Riit, if I am Rong, and misspell it.

J-[_] Justice Demands that our Spelling Method is Simplified, if we are going to Establish **"The New RIGHTEOUS One-World Government,"** whereby all People will be Able to Communicate in the same Language, and thus Avoid any Massive Confusion.

K-[_] King Jesus will get all of that Straightened Out when he Returns in all of his Naked Glory in the Dark Awesome Rolling Clouds of a FEARSOME Sky, along with tens of thousands of his Holy Angels, who will be Flying Inside of those Flying Saucers, which will be Zipping around like Lightning Striking! †§‡

L-[_] Lots of Laughs! King Jesus will be no less than 400 feet Tall, riding his Great White Horse, just as it states in *the Book of Revelation,* which will make it Possible for every Eye to See him: because, if he were just a normal Man, no one could See him at 2 Miles away from their Eyeballs. Therefore, he will have to be a GIANT of a Man, riding his Great White Horse, which will also be 400 feet Tall, and Clad with Armor, as if Prepared for going to WAR: beCause of having to Deal with the Ignorant Fools in the District of Criminals in **"The BIG White OUTHOUSE on the Not-so-Biblical Capitol DUNGHILL!"** — that is, in Washington, which Outhouse has the 2 Stinking Holes for the Dimwitcrats and Reprobates to Squat on, which STINKS to the Highest Heaven with Ancient Elephant Droppings and Fresh Political Donkey Dung! Yes, if you go in there, in order to Smell Out the Truth of the Matter, it all STINKS: beCause those People have not Bathed themselves in the Refreshing Waters of Life since they were Born — even though they Profess to be "Christians" for the most Part, while Pledging their Allegiance to some Bloody Rag: because of not Studying an Enlightening Book, called: **"The UGLY Scarred Dishonest Face of Poor Old Miserable UNCLE SAM!" (A Memorial Day Legacy!) By The Worldwide People's Revolution!® Book 054.** Indeed, they would do Well to also Study: **"The Great False Economy is now DEBUNKED!" (Adolf Hitler

(The so-called "United States of North America," in Disguise!)

had a much Better Economic System!) By The Worldwide People's Revolution!® Book 053.

M-[_] MONEY is all that those Dimwitcrats and Reprobates are Interested in: beCause they Work for the Military Industrial Congressional Bankers' Complex, which is Secretly Orchestrated by Lying Red JEWS. {See www.Amazon.com for: **"Are we Tax Slaves of a Lower Order than Lying Red JEWS?" (HOW to be Liberated from all Slavery, Worldwide!) By The Worldwide People's Revolution!®** Book 052.}

N-[_] Not everyone is Interested in Buying a hundreds Uninspired Books, just to Learn a few things about Lying Red Jews, which they can read all about in the *Holy Bible,* which makes it Perfectly Clear that there are certain Jews who CALL themselves Jews; but, in Reality, they are NOT Israelites! {See *Revelation 2:9 and 3:9, King James Version (KJV),* which is the Authorized Version, which is the ONE and ONLY Correct Version to Study with a Capital S, even though it does not Capitalize all such Important Words as **"The Seven Basic Spiritual Building Blocks of LIFE!" (Faith Hope Trust Love Patience Persistence and Obedience!) By The Worldwide People's Revolution!®** Book 036.}

O-[_] Are there no OPTIONS to Choose from? Must we all get ourselves Greatly Confused by Study ONE Proper Translation, which is, for Example: **"Thu Nq MAGNUFIID Verzhun uv Thu PROVERBZ uv KING SOLUMUN in Plaan Ingglish!"** — which makes all of the Proverbs of King Solomon Understandable, which Book is Inspired by Almighty GOD? †§‡§§

P-[_] Most People are Aware that God has Forsaken this World, and left it in the Care of Satan, our Evil Stepfather: beCause of our Rejections of Truths without any Justifiable Causes, whereby we have become Sons of Perdition, and Daughters of the Devil. †§‡

Q-[_] The Great Question is this: **"Will the Divided States of United Lies be Saved from the Wrath to Come, when the Just Judge Arises to SHAKE TERRIBLY the Whole Earth, whereby every High Tower will FALL, just as Isaiah Reported in his Prophecy about these Last Days?"** {See www.Amazon.com for: **"The Secret City of the Great King!" (HOW the True Church will Escape from the Great Tribulation!) By The Worldwide People's Revolution!®** Book 042. See also Chapter 16-044.}

R-[_] Righteous People will be Blest under all Circumstances, even if they are Flying in Airplanes that Crash into Fields near Shanksville, Pennsylvania, which leave no Airplane Parts, no Bodies, no Blood, no Guts, no Luggage, no Suitcases, no Seats, no Cockpits, no Fuselages, nor any Evidences that any such Airplanes Crashed there, whereby only a small Hole was Discovered in the Ground, which was about 20 feet long, 10 feet wide, and 6 feet deep, which the Federal Burden of Investigation (FBI) said was Proof that 49 People Died there: because the Airplane struck the Ground with such FORCE at 600+ Miles per Hour (MpH), that it VAPORIZED the 6-ton Titanium Jet Engines! Yes, just Try to Imagine HOW that might Happen, which also Vaporized 18,000 Gallons of Jet Fuel, whereby there was NO Fire at the "Crash Site," which was a World Record Event: beCause no Airplane before nor afterwards has ever Vaporized all of its Fuel, whereby there was no Fire at the Crash Site, much less no Bodies, no Blood, no Guts, nor any Visible Airplane Parts, nor even a Diamond Ring — much less an All-American Smiling Tampon! Nevertheless, that is the Official Government Record, which you can read about in *Wickedpedia.* †§‡§§

S-[_] I much Prefer to Study my *Holy Bible,* which has no less than 10,000 Grammatical Errors in it. For Example, in the Lord's Prayer it states, *"Our Father who are in Heaven, ...,"* which should be *"Our Fathers who are in Heaven,"* or *"Our Father who is in Heaven, hallowed is your Holy Name. May your Holy Kingdom Come to the Earth, and your Will be Done on the Earth, even as it is now Done in Heavenly Places."* Yes, there are any number of Improvements that could be made with all such Mutilated Words, whereby we could Heroize the Lord Jesus Properly, and thus MAGNIFY his Inspired Words of Provable Truths for the Innocent Children to Study, whereby they might not Grow Up into Potential Criminals like that Saddam Insane Hussein and Osama bin Laden, who Orchestrated the Evil Events of September 11th, 2001, from a Cave in Afghanistan by Remote Control. Yes, some People say that it was SATAN who Inspired it, who was Working THROUGH Osama bin Laden, who Rounded Up 19 Hijackers from Saudi Arabia and Egypt, who had ZERO Training in Flying HUGE Boeing 747 Airplanes, which they Supposedly Hijacked with Box Cutters in their Hands, and Flew into the Twin World Trade Center Towers 1 and 2 in New Yuck City, which Caused them and Tower 7 to Collapse in less than 10 Seconds: beCause all 283 Hardened Steel Columns Kindly Yielded to the Temptation to COLLAPSE and VAPORIZE on the way down, whereby a few Truckloads of Metal Survived, only to be quickly Scooped Up by the Central Unintelligent Agencies (CIA), and Whisked Away to China and India: so as to Destroy the Evidences as Quickly as Physically Possible, lest it should be Proven that Satan was Actually at Work over there with Nano-Thermite, which can get 4000 °F in less than 2 Seconds, which was used to Slice OFF those Steel Columns, many of which were 22-inches by 52-inches, and as Tall as those Buildings, being Welded and Bolted to tens of thousands of Trusses — all of which Yielded to the Temptation to COLLAPSE like Ballet Dancers, hitting the Floor at the very same Instant, in UNISON: beCause that is what all such Hardened Steel Columns Naturally DO when they are Spooked by Satanic People like Osama bin Laden with Long Beards, like Pirates on the High Seas! Yes, you may not Believe it, even as I do not Believe it; but, that is the Official Record in the District of Criminals, which is a bit more Reliable than the President Kennedy Assassination Cover-up Report by the Warren Commission: beCause *THE 9/11 COMMISSION REPORT* did not even Mention World Trade Center (WTC) Tower 7 in its first Report: because it was the Headquarters for the Mayor of New York City, as well as the Headquarters for the FBI, CIA, BATF, FEMA, and more than 20 Major Banks and Insurance Companies, being the Center of Attraction, you might say, which had no less than 400 Billion SOLID GOLD BRICKS Stored in the Vaults in the Basement, which the Snooze Reporters never even MENTIONED: beCause that News was not Sensational enough for them to Report about. †§‡§§ {See www.AE911TRUTH.org for a Mountain of Evidence against the Outlandish LIES of the Cover-up Federal Government. Also see YouTube Videos by Dr. Judy Wood, who has no Cause for Telling any Outlandish Lies, who, along with the Honest Architects and Engineers, should be Rewarded with **"Beautiful Swanky PALACES!" (A New Concept in Living Habits!) By The Worldwide People's Revolution!® Book 066.**}

(The so-called "United States of North America," in Disguise!)

T-[_] Did not NIST (National Institute of Sciences and Technologies) Discover any Military-grade Nano-Thermite at any of those Crash Sites in New Yuck City? Would their 3,000+ Scientists not Notice any Evidence concerning what Actually Happened, when they made a "Thorough Investigation" of the Scenes of the Crimes, 5 Years after the Fact?

U-[_] You must Try to Understand that the Evidences at the Crash Sites were all Swept Up and Mopped Up and Washed Away by the Time that NIST got its Ass Out of Bed, some 5 Years after September 11th, 2001: beCause the Federal Government, under the Administration of President George Warmonger Bush and Little Dick Chicanery, Incorporated, did not Call for an Investigation until 4 Years LATER: beCause they were Certain that Osama bin Laden and Saddam Hussein had done it with the Help of those Patsy Hijackers from Saudi Arabia, most of whom are still Alive! †§‡

V-[_] I was another Victim of the Evil Events of September 11th, 2001.

W-[_] Will you ever get any Justice? Will George Warmonger Bush and Little Dick Chicanery be brought to Trial for their Roles in that Grand False Flag Operation and their War Crimes? Will, Larry Silverstein ever be brought to Trial for his Cover-up Lies, being the Proud Owner of the World Trade Center Towers, for which he got 6 Billion Dollars-worth of Insurance, just 6 Months before the "incident"?

X-[_] X-amount of Red Jew Bankers must have been in on the Conspiracy, who must have Removed their Gold from the Basement of WTC 7, before September 11th, 2001. Otherwise, the News Media would have Surely Mention how they Rescued it, most of which was German Gold. Did the Germans say nothing? Was that Gold not Sensational enough to even Mention it on Snooze Reports? †§‡

Y-[_] You must not have Seen Yesterday's News Reports about it. Indeed, I Heard that Little Green Men from Mars were down there in those Bank Vaults, Cleaning House, which is WHY the News Media did not Mention the Stash of Gold that was Stored there: beCause it was none of our Business. Yes, it was Classified TOP SECRET by the Central Unintelligent Agencies (CIA), who also never Recorded anything about that Gold, which they might have Hidden in the Pentagon for the Time when the Kennedy Papers will be Revealed, in the Year 4040. †§‡§§

Z-[_] The ZEAL of **The Worldwide People's Revolution!**® will Change all of that.

01-04 [_] O Elected King, that is some Serious Stuff that should be Thoroughly Investigated by Unbiased Foreign Nations — such as Germany, Sweden, Switzerland, Norway, Denmark, Russia, China, India, and whomever might be Interested. After all, we American Tax Slaves Wasted 10 Times as much Money on Investigating the Adulteries of the President Bill MOANica LEWDwinsky Clinton Scandal, and came up with nothing but a Sperm-Stained Dress. †§‡§§

01-05 [_] I much Prefer to Bury the Hatchet, and Forget about all Past American Sins. After all, even if those Lying Red Jews gained some 2 Trillion Dollars from it all, so what? Indeed, it provided a Good Excuse for getting RID of that Wicked WICKED Saddam Hussein, whereby

ISIS (Israeli Secret Instigation Services) could be Born, whereby we might have "Eternal" Wars in the Middle East, whereby Red Jew Weapons Manufacturers might gain hundreds of Billions of Dollars. Yes, they are the GOOD Guys, whom we should all LOVE: beCause, without those Lovable Gory Wars, none of us would have any JOBS! Therefore, Thank God for those Red Jews, who keep us Honest White Jews Working. Yes, Thank God for the Military Industrial Congressional Bankers' Complex Economy, which Relies on LIES and Deceptions, which has no Use for Truths, much less the Wisdom of King Solomon, who would put us to Work, Building those **"GLORIOUS Swanky Hotels Castles and Fortresses!" (Beautiful Planned City States for WISE Intelligent Well-Educated People with Common Sense and Good Understanding!) By The Worldwide People's Revolution!®** Book 019. †§‡§§

01-06 [_] This Book is far too Sarcastic for my Tastes. I much Prefer *The Adventures of Tom Sawyer and Huckleberry Finn,* which did not Reveal **"HOW to Bring those Terrorist Attacks to a Screeching HALT!" (Terrorists Beware that your Days are Numbered!) By The Worldwide People's Revolution!®** Book 043. †§‡

01-07 [_] You have the Titles turned around backwards. The Book is called: **"Terrorists Beware that your Days are Numbered!"** Indeed, **"The Swanky Sword of Divine Truths"** will make that Possible at: **"The Great Worldwide TELEVISED Court HEARING,"** when all of the Leaders of all Major Nations will be Gathered Together in Saint Peter's Basilica, in Rome, where our Elected King may Ask them a few Important Questions, which are Outlined in the above mentioned Book, which everyone in the World should Study with an Open Mind: beCause this Madness is about to be brought to an END!

01-08 [_] I can hardly Wait for that Glorious Day. {See www.Amazon.com for: **"The END of CONFUSION!" (The Great CELEBRATION of the Magnificent Wedding of the Humble Honest Nations, and the Grand Year of JUBILEE!) By The Worldwide People's Revolution!®** Book 050.

01-09 [_] You can Hasten it by Sowing the Seeds of Truths in the Gardens of other People's Lives, beginning with: **"The New RIGHTEOUS One-World Government!" (HOW to Establish a Righteous One-World Government without Going to WAR!) By The Worldwide People's Revolution!®** Book 056.

01-10 [_] I would Love to Help you out, O Elected King; but, I am far too Poor to Afford to Buy any of your Books to Sell at a Reasonable Price. For Example, if I had to Pay 6$ for each Copy of the above mentioned Book, I would have to Sell them for at least 7$, just to make any Profit, even though I will Confess that it is well Worth at least 10$, seeing that it is much more Satisfying than any Meal of Hog Slop or Dog Food at the Death and Hell Restaurant. Indeed, it is just a small Book; but, it comes with Powerful Punches in the Guts of the Evil Empire, which, like this Inspired Book, has all of the Potential of putting that Wicked Uncle Sam in his Cold Dark Grave near General Robert E. Lee's House in the Arlington Cemetery, in Virginia, if he does not Thoroughly REPENT, and Change his Ways of Living. Yes, he should Know by now that his Bloody Dirty NASTY Filthy STINKING Underwear has been Exposed for what it is. However, if the Masses of People do not get to Read all such Inspired Books, they will never come to Appreciate the Beauty of them, much less get to Live in: **"The Environmentalists' Paradise!"** Book 035.

(The so-called "United States of North America," in Disguise!)

— Chapter 02 —

Why are the Eyeballs of Uncle Sam Crossed?

02-01 [_] Well, it is likely beCAUSE he has one Eye on Money, and the other Eye on his Grave, which keeps him Worried. After all, his Sins are Bound to be Discovered by the Masses of People, sooner or later, who will Forsake him in Favor of **"The New RIGHTEOUS One-World Government,"** which is a far Superior Plan: beCause that would provide a Way for almost everyone in the World to become Moderately RICH, and without Telling any Lies, nor Selling any Trash, which would make most People Extremely Happy, and especially after moving into those **"Beautiful Swanky PALACES!" (A New Concept in Living Habits!) By The Worldwide People's Revolution!®** Book 066.

02-02 [_] O Elected King, if there is anything that Americans FEAR, it is the Establishment of a ONE-WORLD Government, which Means that we would Lose our Sovereignty. †§‡

02-03 [_] That is Pure Nonsense. No Nation would Lose its Sovereignty: because each Nation would still be Responsible for Defending itself, even as each Swanky Fortress would also be Responsible for Defending itself and Governing itself, which would greatly Reduce the Need for any Monster Federal Government in **The Divided States of United Lies,** which would mostly be Abandoned: because those Swanky Fortresses would be Designed for Defense, whereby they would have very little Need for any Federal Government, except to Attend to National Parks, and whatever is Outside of those Fortresses.

02-04 [_] O King, this is the first of your Inspired Books that I have "red," and therefore, I have no Idea what you are Talking about.

02-05 [_] Well, you are like the 12-year-old Boy, who began to read the *Bible* in the Book of *Matthew,* instead of *Genesis,* which tells about what Happened in the Beginning, according to the Hebrew MYTH, which many Jews, Muslims, and Christians Profess to Believe: beCause they have Faith in all such Fairy Tales, as the Apostle Paul called them. (See *Titus 1:14, KJV.*) Yes, he referred to them as *Jewish Fables,* which is Exactly what they are, which can easily be Proven in a Courtroom, if anyone is Interested in it. {See www.Amazon.com for: **"What is WRong with those Professing Christians?" (A Self-Examination of the Heart of the Body of Good Government!),** Book 002, plus: **"For the Love of Money!" (The Strange Things that People Say and Do to Get more Money!) By The Worldwide People's Revolution!®** Book 003.}

02-06 [_] O King, if the Noah's Ark Story is a Jewish Fabrication, which was taken from an Ancient Babylonian Myth, it is Understandable why Jesus would Refer to it and Noah, as if they were for Real: because the Jews Sincerely came to Believe all such Fairy Tales, even as most Americans have come to Believe that 19 Hijackers did all of the Marvelous Things that they supposedly did during September 11th, 2001. For Example, an Untrained Pilot, who had never Flown a large Passenger Airplane, supposedly took over the Plane at 22,000 feet up in the Sky, and dropped it down to Ground Zero in less then 7 Minutes, while going around a 180° Curve over Washington, D.C., and got it Lined Up with the Pentagon, Perfectly, while just barely missing a Freeway, Light Posts, and Trees, whereby his 45-feet-wide Airplane made a 16-feet-wide Hole in the Previously Hardened Concrete Wall, which was the most Secure Part of the entire Building; but, left NO Holes for each of the 6-ton Titanium Jet Engines! In Fact, not even the Windows were Broken Out where the Engines should have Plowed into the Wall. Therefore, that Hijacker must have figured out HOW to SHRINK DOWN the whole Airplane, just to make it FIT into that 16-feet-wide Hole, Wings, Engines, and ALL! Yes, that Hijacker was a True Magician, you might say, who also Caused the "Black Boxes" to Disappear in all 4 "Airplanes" that supposedly Crashed during that Day of Woes, which was an Extraordinary Feat, I would say, seeing that those Black Boxes have been Recovered from nearly every Airplane Crash since they were put into Use, including the Plane that Crashed in the Ukraine, and the other French one that Crashed over the Atlantic Ocean, even after its Beeper quit; but, NOT in the Case of the Airplane that Crashed into that Field near Shank's Village, in Pennsylvania, which simply VANISHED, along with 49 Bodies, Blood, Guts, and all Parts of the Airplane, even as someone Previously Pointed Out in this Insane Book, which should be Gathered Up from the 4 Corners of the Earth, and BURNED, lest some Ignorant Children might Discover it, and then Lose Faith in Buzzeldick the Great, or even in Uncle Sam, who is the most Trustworthy of all Government Officials, Worldwide. Yes, you might Remember the Chelsee Maning and Edward Snowden WickedLeaks, which Exposed some of Uncle Sam's Bloody Underwear. †§‡§§

02-07 [_] Well, it does seem that Jesus made no Effort at all to Correct anything in the *Holy Bible:* beCause he did not Object to leaving People in their States of Ignorance: beCause he is only Interested in Discovering the Most Intelligent People to Govern this World with him, during the Future; and therefore, if someone Believes some Outlandish LIE — such as Noah getting enough Fresh Water into the Ark to Water 28,000+ Bovines, Daily, and also Clean up after them — then it is for Certain that such a Person is NOT Qualified to Govern this World with him! Therefore, all such Jewish Fables are left in the Books just for the Purpose of SIFTING OUT the Stupid People, and I do Mean REALLY STUPID Ignorant FOOLS! †§‡

02-08 [_] O King, I do Wish to God that I could Learn ALL of the Facts, whereby I might Rightly Judge all such Important Subjects.

02-09 [_] Well, you are an Exceptionally Intelligent Person, who might even Qualify to Enter into the Holy Kingdom of All that is GOOD: beCause of having Good Judgment. Indeed, no one with any less Love for the Whole Truth will have any Place within that Holy Kingdom. Therefore, Keep an Open Mind, and be Willing to Change your Mind at any Time: beCause we could all be Proven to be WRong about a LOT of Important Subjects at **"The Great Worldwide TELEVISED Court HEARING!" (That Great Meeting of the Most Intelligent Minds!) By The Worldwide People's Revolution!® Book 041.**

02-10 [_] O King, I must Confess that I do not Understand the Master Plan of the Master Farmer. WHY would God Allow Humanity to go on Suffering for thousands of Years, if he Exists? Why does he not just come down here from Heaven, or from wherever he is Hiding himself, and thus Prove that he is the Great Creator God, whereby we might all become Believers? Why is he Testing our Faith in him?

— Chapter 03 —

WHY God has not Revealed himself to Humanity!

03-01 [_] God has Revealed himself to Humanity through Jesus Christ, who came to Prepare the Way for the Coming Kingdom or Good Government of the Gods, who will Establish their Righteous One-World Government over all of the Nations at the End of the Ages, after we Human Beings have Learned our Lessons, and have Proven to ourselves that we are Incapable of Governing ourselves Apart from the Divine Laws of the Gods, who have one Mind, one Heart, one Great Purpose, and one Great Goal, which is to Establish their Holy Kingdom over all of the Multitudes of Worlds within this Vast Universe, which has Billions of TRILLIONS of Worlds: beCause the Creations of the Gods go on and on, forever and ever: beCause that is the WORK of the Gods, which some Ignorant Fools Disagree with; but, that is only beCause they have never Met with Moses, Elijah, Jesus, nor John, who is still among us, who may Visit whomever is Worthy of his Visitation, who has Purified his Mind and Body by Means of Fasting and Praying, even as all of the Holy Prophets did. (See *Deuteronomy 9:9 and 18; First Kings 17—19; and Matthew 4, KJV.*)

03-02 [_] Well, if that is True, most Professing "Christians" have Certainly Missed the Mark, as the Apostle Paul might say: beCause they are about as Holy as MUD, you might say, which has been Soaked in Used Motor Oil. After all, most of them Vainly Imagine that there will be Stinking Noisy Polluting CARS in the Holy Kingdom of All that is GOOD, as if Jesus would Prefer to Ride in a Stinking Car, rather than WALK, or Ride a Horse. Indeed, just beCause *they* are Fat and Lazy, it does not Mean that any of the *Saints* are. (See *Revelation 19:11—16.*)

03-03 [_] Are you saying that all Saints are Healthy and Strong, like Moses was when he "Died"? (See *Deuteronomy 34:7.*)

03-04 [_] Well, if you Vainly Imagine that Jesus Christ and all of his Self-disciplined Disciples were/are Sickly and Diseased, you have Completely Misjudged what the *Scriptures* Teach. Indeed, Jesus said, *"... I am come so that you might have Good Health, and have it more Abundantly." — John 10:10, NMV.*

03-05 [_] So, if that is True, WHY are so many professing "Christians" so SICK and Diseased?

03-06 [_] Well, they Forgot to Study *Psalm 103:1—5,* in the New MAGNIFIED Version, which makes it Perfectly Clear that we can be Healed from ALL of our Diseases; but, only IF we Truly REPENT. {See www.Amazon.com for: **"HOW to Become a HOLY Man!" (40 Good Reasons WHY People Should FAST and PRAY!), Book 045, plus: "The Proper RULES for FASTING!" (The Complete Instruction Manual for True Repentance!) By The Worldwide People's Revolution!® Book 046.**}

03-07 [_] We must be Saved by GRACE, and not by Works, lest any Man should Boast about it. For Example, when a Doctor Knife Cuts Out a 25-pound Tumor that is Lodged in some Fat

Lady's Bowels, he is Saving her by the GRACE of GOD, and NOT by any Works, lest he might be able to Boast about it. †§‡ (See *Ephesians 2:8—10, KJV*.)

03-08 [_] You must have been Raised in the Unholy Church of Little Faith on Lonesome Street and Suicide Avenue: beCause you completely Missed the Message in *Second Corinthians 7:1* — *"Therefore, having those Promises, dearly Beloved — that God's Holy Spirit will Live within us, if we are Holy, even as he is Holy — let us Cleanse ourselves from all Filthiness of the Flesh and Spirit, while Perfecting ourselves in Holiness in the Fear of God, who will only Accept those Most Holy People into his Holy Kingdom."* — NMV.

03-09 [_] O Elected King, that is NOT how my *Bible* reads; and therefore, it is just another LIE? Therefore, you should be Tried in a Courtroom, and Sentenced to DEATH for Telling all such LIES! †§‡

03-10 [_] Well, you did not point out any Specific Lies within that Verse of Provable Truths; and therefore, you are in Danger of being Cast into Hellfire for your False Accusations. Indeed, I already told you that there are well over 200 Different Translations of the *Scriptures*. Therefore, if you Study Chapter 6 of Second Corinthians, you will Discover that the Verse is in Context with that Chapter. In other Words, *Second Corinthians 7:1* should have been Included in Chapter 6: beCause it is a Continuation of those Good Thoughts, which the Translators apparently did not Discover, unto their own Great Shame during the Day of Judgment. Moreover, it is also very likely that certain Words were also Carefully Removed from that "Book": because Lying Red Jews do not Want the Masses of People to Discover the Whole Truth about any Subject. †§‡ {See www.Amazon.com for: **"Are we Tax Slaves of a Lower Order than Lying Red JEWS?" (HOW to be Liberated from Tax Slavery, Worldwide!) By The Worldwide People's Revolution!® Book 052.**}

— Chapter 04 —

"Many are Called; but, Few are Chosen!"

04-01 [_] O Elected King, are YOU one of the Chosen Ones? Moreover, if you are, what are you Chosen FOR?

04-02 [_] Well, it is Obvious that I was Chosen to Write more than 350 Inspired Books: beCause I have the Evidence to Prove it; but, whether or not I am Chosen for any Position in the Kingdom of the Gods is another Subject. I Seriously Doubt that I am. In Fact, I might be one of the Last People to Enter into it: beCause of not Living up to my own Nolij.

04-03 [_] So, O King, if you do not Qualify for that Holy Kingdom, WHO DOES? Indeed, I would Think that you would be a Chief Servant in the Kingdom of God, just for Writing so many Good Books.

(The so-called "United States of North America," in Disguise!)

04-04 [_] Well, I would say that there are many Positions to be Filled within the Kingdom; and therefore, it is Possible that I could be an Author during the Future, even in the Kingdom of God on this Earth. After all, very few People have been as Faithful as I have been to Write the Inspired Words of Provable Truths that God has Blest me with.

04-05 [_] So, will any of those Wicked Lying Politicians in Washington, District of Criminals, enter into the Kingdom of God, O King?

04-06 [_] Well, that is for God to Judge. After all, I do not Personally Know any of them; and therefore, I cannot Rightly Judge any of them. However, as a General Rule, very few People will Qualify for any such Positions: because one must be HOLY in Mind, Spirit, and BODY, even as Moses and Elijah were Holy, which Means that Jesus was Correct, when he said: *"Strive to Enter in at the Strait Gate: because many People, I tell you, will Seek to Enter into the Government of God, which is made up of Great Kings and their Queens; but, most People shall not be Able to Overcome their Sins, and Stop Sinning: beCause Broad and Wide is the Way that Leads to Self-destruction, and many People go in that Broadway, which is Filled with all Kinds of Temptations and Lusts, whereby Satan Entices them to Sin, and to Disobey the Dietary Laws, even as he Tempted Mother Eve, whereby they make Fools of themselves, and even Return to Eat their own Vomit, as the Proverb states: because they are Overcome by their Lusts or Longing Desires for Vain Things that cannot Satisfy the Soul. Nevertheless, if a Man should Humble himself by Means of Fasting and Praying, until he becomes like an Innocent Child with a Purified Mind and Body, he may Enter into the Holy Kingdom of All that is Good; but, only if he Sacrifices everything except the Basic Necessities of Life. Yes, he must be Contented with Foods and Clothing, and whatever the Church Provides for him: because his Goal is to Obtain a Position in the Government of God, not Countless Possessions and Vain Things. Therefore, let him Sell whatever Possessions that he has, and give his Wealth to those People who have none, and then come and Follow after me, all of the Way to the Torture Stake, if he Wants a Position with me in the Kingdom, which might seem to be a bit Radical or Extreme; but, I Assure you that it will Separate the Men of God from the Sons of Satan, in as much as they Love and Obey my Commandments. However, that is not to say that everyone who Follows me will be Crucified for it; but, they will most Definitely be Persecuted and Tormented by the Unbelievers for it, whereby they will be Qualified for a Better Reward than those People who make no such Sacrifices, who even become Moneymongers and Whoremongers, and Forget about their First Love for me, whereby they Promised to Love and Obey my Commandments, whereby they might be Healthy and Happy, like me."* — NMV of Matthew 7:13—14.

04-07 [_] So, was Jesus saying that we did not Need the ADA (American Disability Act)? What about ObamaScare — was it not Needed for Providing Good Health?

04-08 [_] Well, you may Interpret it in any Way that you Like; but, I Seriously Doubt that most People will pay much Attention to it: because they cannot Find it within their Unholy Mutilated Bibles. However, I have not needed the Services of Medical Doctors in more than 50 Years, nor have I used any MediSINZ during all of that Time. Moreover, I can Honestly say that I do not have a Pain within my entire Body. Therefore, the Teachings of Jesus Christ have Served me Well, you might say; but, only beCause of my Unique Interpretations of them, which some People say is Pure Blasphemy! Yes, they are the ones who are Suffering with all Kinds of Ailments, and have no Idea what to Do about them. Moreover, they are far too Proud to read any of my Inspired Books: because Satan has Obviously Deceived them, and Blinded their Minds: so that they cannot See the Light of Truths.

04-09 [_] O Elected King, they might not See nor Understand the Truths in this World of Wonders, in the same Way that you See and Understand them: beCause everyone has a Different Perspective, whereby they draw up their Conclusions in Different Ways, which may be Equally as Correct as your Conclusions.

04-10 [_] Well, all of our Beliefs can be Proven to be True or False at **"The Great Worldwide TELEVISED Court HEARING!"** — that is, IF anyone has any Interest in Proving him or herself to be WRong about almost all of his or her Beliefs, unless they Agree with mine, which are Based on Facts. For Example, Voting for one of 2 or 3 or more WRong Political Parties will not Solve our Massive Problems: beCause, Voting, itself, has no Magic Powers to make Things RIIT.

— Chapter 05 —

The Insanity of Election Deceptions!

05-01 [_] **The Divided States of United Lies** is Famous for its Election Deceptions, whereby at least 3/4ths of the People are Dissatisfied with their Elected Officials: beCause no President has ever Represented them in Washington, District of Criminals. Indeed, for that Reason and many others, not even half of the People bother themselves to Vote for Presidents: beCause they Know for a Fact that it is all Rigged by the Oligarchy, which is otherwise known as the Military Industrial Congressional Bankers' Complex, whose Big Chiefs are those Lying Red Jew Bankers, who Control the Great False Economy, who have Arranged for their own "Eternal Enrichment," whereby American Tax Slaves and Usury Slaves are in Debt to them by no less than 150 Trillion Dollars, which, if Stacked Up in 100-dollar Bills, would reach half way to the MOON! And yet Politicians continually Brag that the United States of America is the Great Nation on the Earth, which should be Revised to read: "The Divided States of United Lies is the most Indebted Nation on the Earth." Nevertheless, many Americans still Hope that Voting for 2 Wrong Political Parties will somehow Fix it.

05-02 [_] O Elected King, if we Americans were Wise, we would Vote for YOU, who would Persuade those Lying Red Jews to FORGIVE us of all Debts, and Celebrate the Great Year of JUBILEE, even as Moses Taught in *Leviticus 25*. However, it is very Unlikely that your Name will ever Appear on any Ballots, in spite of the Fact that no one Challenges your Kingship! Indeed, you have Zero Opposition: beCause no one is Willing to Stand Up Against you: beCause they Fear **"The Swanky Sword of Divine Truths," (The Most Powerful Weapon in the Whole Universe!)**, Book 067, which they cannot Withstand with their Weak Flimsy Rubber Swords, which they should Trash, before they Cut Off their own Heads, which are full of Capitalist Lies and Deceptions.

(The so-called "United States of North America," in Disguise!)

05-03 [_] Well, if you have Listened to the Presidential Election Campaigns of both Major Political Parties, you have probably noticed that they have one Major Thing in Common, which is a Promise of Positive Changes, which is followed by a List of Things that they are going to do for us Tax Slaves, which is Based on the Assumption that the CONgress will go along with their Proposals, which they seldom do: beCause they are Controlled by the Military Industrial Congressional Bankers' Complex. Therefore, if it does not Fit into their Agendas, it is not likely to become a Reality by any Means. Therefore, all such Promises are like Balloons, which are simply full of hot Air, and may Float around for awhile, and even seem to Cheer Up X-amount of Ignorant People, who have Hope in all such Promises, who are Historically Disappointed in most Cases. Meanwhile, most everything seems to be getting Worse and WORSE, even as Americans in general seem to be getting Fatter and FATTER! Meanwhile, the Highways and Bridges are in Worse Conditions than ever: because all of those Pot Holes mean that more Vehicles are being Damaged, whereby more Vehicles must be Repaired and/or Replaced with New Vehicles, which is Good for Car Sales, which is Good for Bankers who Loan Money for Buying them, which is also Good for the Manufacturers of Automobiles; but, it is NOT Good for the Normal Work Slaves, who have to Suffer with the Consequences of a Neglectful Government, which has always been "Short on Money." Yes, as far back as I can Remember, no Government ever had as much Money as it Needed for doing things Correctly — such as Building Good Stone Bridges, like the Romans Built, which are still Standing Strong. ‡

05-04 [_] O Elected King, it is our Bad Health that is going to Destroy America: because that is Costing us more than 4 Trillion Dollars per Year, which is like Flushing our Money down Toilet Drains: because those Drugs are not Healing us from whatever Ails us. ‡

05-05 [_] Well, the Best Solution for the Health Care Problem is to PREVENT Sicknesses and Diseases and Degenerated Children, by Living on Natural Wholesome Foods, as Opposed to Trying to Live on Imitation Foods, Highly-processed Foods, Junk Foods, Poisoned Foods, Devitalized Foods, Demineralized Foods, Plastic Foods, and all Kinds of Poisonous Drinks and Countless Drugs, Preservatives, Pesticides, Herbicides, Fly Sprays, and whatever might be in or on all such Foods and Drinks, including those Genetically-modified Foods, which Europeans have Outlawed: because they have Learned that Capitalist Americans cannot be Trusted. ‡

05-06 [_] So, O Elected King, are you saying that we could Save TRILLIONS of Dollars, just by PREVENTING our Sicknesses and Diseases, even as we can Prevent House Fires and Tornado Destructions by Building Proper Stone Houses, like the Pantheon, in Rome? Would that not Require at least 20 Years to Accomplish it?

05-07 [_] Well, it all Depends on HOW we go about Doing it, and how Quickly People Change their Minds about their Present False Economy and BAD Lifestyles, whereby they are now going to Hell, you might say, while Imaging that they are "the greatest nation on the earth," which has only Built Up their Destructive PRIDE, which has Blinded their Minds, whereby most Americans cannot even bring themselves around to Confess that they are in a Living Hell, being Trapped by the Devil, himself. Indeed, just HOW could any of them Escape from their Slavery, Lies, and Election Deceptions?

05-08 [_] O Elected King, when People become so Deceived as Americans, they are a Lost Cause. Indeed, there is no Way that anyone can Save them from their Madness: because they

Refuse to Recognize their Basic Foundational Problems, which are Religious, Spiritual, Social, Moral, and Political Problems, which we can Blame onto False Preachers and Misguided Teachers, who, for the most part, are not even Aware that they are Teaching Lies and Deceptions. For Example, Politicians often talk about Uniting the People, as if it were Possible and Practical to UNITE People who are like Sheeps and Goats with People who are like Lions and Wolves, who have Contrary Natures. Indeed, the Prophet Daniel likened it to an Attempt to Mix Iron with Clay, or Oil with Water, which simply do NOT Mix Together. Nevertheless, X-amount of People are Determined to make them Mix Together: because they Visualize a World that has everyone in Perfect Harmony, as if they were all Sheeps, or all Goats, with no Wolves nor Lions among them, which is Unrealistic. Indeed, in Reality, there are X-amount of BAD People among us, who must be SEPARATED from the Good People, who can be Discovered by Filling Out and Filing **"The Complete SURVEYS of our VALUES,"** on the Internet. In other Words, the GOOD People, or the RIGHTEOUS People, who Want to Say and Do what is RIGHT and Good for themselves and others, must Study the Surveys of our Values, and Check the Appropriate Boxes, whereby they can Discover other People of Like-mindedness, who must then be HIRED by **"The New RIGHTEOUS One-World Government"** to Build their own **"GLORIOUS Swanky Hotels Castles and Fortresses,"** whereby they can Live in PEACE, without any Loans, without any Interest, and without any Taxes. Moreover, whomever Objects to that Plan is Suspect of being an Enemy of some Kind, who is Seeking to take Advantage of other People, rather than Bear his own Burdens, which everyone should Bear, at least until they are too Old to do so. †‡

05-09 [_] Well, if the Masses of People Learned about such a Good Government, they could simply VOTE for it to be Established, and thus Solve any Problems for RIGHTEOUS People; but, what about the "99.999,999,999%" of the People, who are Unrighteous, who do not even Believe in Jesus Christ, according to his Teachings? ‡

05-10 [_] O Elected King, I am not Aware that 99.999+% of the People are Unrighteous. Are you Sure that they cannot be Converted? Can they not Change their Minds, and Live Righteous Lives? Are they ALL Thieves, Liars, Robbers, Spiritual Murderers, Spiritual Adulterers, Spiritual Whoremongers, Drug Addicts, Gluttons, Drunkards, and FOOLS?

(The so-called "United States of North America," in Disguise!)

— Chapter 06 —

Just how RIGHTEOUS are the Masses of People?

06-01 [_] Well, if you took the Following Poll on the Streets of New York City, you would quickly Discover the Answer to the above Question, which would not likely Surprise you by any Means: because you would likely Check the same Boxes with X's.

    A-[_] Do you Believe that most Americans are Honest Righteous People?
        1-[_] Yes, 2-[_] No, 3-[_] Maybe, 4-[_] have no Idea.

    B-[_] Would you Trust the Normal American to Manage your Bank Account for you?
        1-[_] Yes, 2-[_] No, 3-[_] Maybe, 4-[_] I have no Bank Account.

    C-[_] Do you Believe that most Americans would Answer the Questions Honestly in **"The SURVEYS of our VALUES,"** if they knew that they could get to Live in **"Beautiful Swanky PALACES"** for doing so?
        1-[_] Yes, 2-[_] No, 3-[_] I Doubt they would, 4-[_] I do not Understand the Question, 5-[_] It would Depend on whether or not they Believed that they might be Caught Lying.

    D-[_] Would you Trust your own Spouse with a Million Dollars in Cash?
        1-[_] Yes, 2-[_] No, 3-[_] Maybe, 4-[_] I have no Spouse.

    E-[_] Do you Trust Elected Officials in the Federal Government?
        1-[_] Yes, 2-[_] No, 3-[_] Maybe, 4-[_] Some of them, 5-[_] One of them.

    F-[_] Do you Trust Elected Officials in the State Government?
        1-[_] Yes, 2-[_] No, 3-[_] Maybe, 4-[_] Sometimes, 6-[_] Most of the Time.

    G-[_] Do you Believe that most Americans would do what is Right in the Eyes of God, if they should Learn what is Riit in the Eyes of God?
        1-[_] Yes, 2-[_] No, 3-[_] Maybe, 4-[_] I do not Understand the Question.

    H-[_] Would you Honestly Answer the Questions in **"The Complete SURVEYS of our VALUES"**?
        1-[_] Yes, 2-[_] No, 3-[_] Maybe, 4-[_] I have never "red" those Surveys.

    I-[_] Would you Attempt to Hide your True Beliefs, if you Answered the Questions in **"The Complete SURVEYS of our VALUES"**?
        1-[_] Yes, 2-[_] No, 3-[_] Maybe, 4-[_] I am Innocent, and have nothing to Hide, 5-[_] I am Guilty, and have much to Hide; but, those Surveys do not Ask Personal Questions about Past nor Present Sins.

J-[_] If you were a Judge, would you Judge Righteously?
   1-[_] Yes, 2-[_] No, 3-[_] Maybe, 4-[_] It would Depend on the Case,
   5-[_] It would Depend on the Color of the Skin of whomever is Charged with a Crime,
   6-[_] It would Depend on whether or not I Liked the Person who is Charged with a Crime,
   7-[_] It would Depend on my Mood at the Time of the Trial,
   8-[_] It would Depend on whether or not someone Bribed me, and for how much Money.

K-[_] If you were Falsely Accused of a Major Crime that you did not Commit, would you Defend yourself, or let the Jury Hang you?
   1-[_] I would Defend myself, and not keep Silent.
   2-[_] I would keep Silent, and let them Hang me.
   3-[_] I would Hire a Good Lawyer to Defend me.
   4-[_] I would do my Best to Kill the False Accuser.
   5-[_] I would Patiently Bear my Cross, even if the Democratic Jury Crucified me.
   6-[_] I would come to the Defense of anyone who is Falsely Accused.
   7-[_] I will go to Heaven, if they Hang me.
   8-[_] I will go to Hell, if they Hang me.
   9-[_] They will never Hang me: because I will keep myself as far away from Societies as Possible, and Live in the Bob Marshal Wilderness of Montana with the Bears and Rattlesnakes: because I am not Crazy. §§

L-[_] If you could Vote for a Righteous King of a Righteous One-World Government, would you Vote for him?
   1-[_] Yes, I would Vote for him. 2-[_] No, I would not Vote for him.
   3-[_] I do not Believe that any such King Exists.
   4-[_] I would Vote for him if he has Filled Out and Filed **"The Complete SURVEYS of our VALUES!"** (SURVEYS of Religious Spiritual Political Governmental Sexual Social Moral Economic Business Labor Habitual and Miscellaneous VALUES!) By The Worldwide People's Revolution!® Book 059.
   5-[_] I would have to Question him, in Person, just to Discover whether or not I might Trust him.
   6-[_] He would have to be Thoroughly Vetted, before I could Vote for him.
   7-[_] He might be a Tyrant in Disguise.
   8-[_] It would all Depend on how Limited his Powers are. {See www.Amazon.com for: **"The CONSTITUTION for the New RIGHTEOUS One-World GovernMint!"** (HOW all Peoples can get True Justice, and Celebrate the Great Year of JUBILEE!) By The Worldwide People's Revolution!® Book 016.
   9-[_] I cannot Imagine a One-World Government being Workable. Indeed, I have never "red" a Book, called: **"The New RIGHTEOUS One-World Government!"** (HOW to Establish a Righteous One-World Government without Going to WAR!) By The Worldwide People's Revolution!® Book 056.

(The so-called "United States of North America," in Disguise!)

M-[_] Can you be Trusted to be a Good Treasurer, who takes Care of the Money?
    1-[_] Yes, 2-[_] No, 3-[_] Maybe, 4-[_] I have never been Tempted by much Money, whereby it might have been Worth Stealing it.

N-[_] Would you Vote for doing away with all Money, if you could Live in **"Beautiful Swanky PALACES!"**?
    1-[_] Yes, 2-[_] No, 3-[_] Maybe,
    4-[_] There are no such Palaces. However, when they come into Existence, I will Vote for doing Away with all Money, which will Solve thousands of Problems.
    5-[_] I am not Afraid of the Criminals who are Produced by the Use of Money.
    6-[_] I cannot Imagine Living without Money. HOW would we Buy anything?
    7-[_] **"The Swanky Associations of Working Soldiers"** would Provide everything that is Needed for a High Standard of Living, and only do an Average of 4 Hours of Common Labor per Day, 6 Days per Week, or the Equivalent thereof, and have the Remainder of the Day for whatever they Want to do.
    8-[_] I do not Believe that such Voluntary Working Soldiers can be Trusted to Provide all of the Good Things that we might Need for a High Standard of Living.
    9-[_] I Promise to "reed" all of the Books that are Listed in Chapter 16: so that I can Qualify to Live in those **"Beautiful Swanky PALACES!"**

O-[_] Would you be Willing to "reed" all of the Books that are Listed in Chapter 16, if you could get to Live in those **"Beautiful Swanky PALACES!"** just for doing it?
    1-[_] Yes, 2-[_] No, 3-[_] Maybe, 4-[_] I will have to Check them out, first.

P-[_] Do you Believe that most People in the World would be Willing to read all of the Books that are Listed in Chapter 16, in their own Languages, if they could Live in those Palaces for doing it?
    1-[_] Yes, I Believe it, 2-[_] No, I do not Believe it, 3-[_] Maybe they would,
    4-[_] They most Definitely would read those Books, if they were Guaranteed such Palaces.
    5-[_] They could still not be Trusted. Even Criminals can read books.

Q-[_] Would you Trust a Person to be an Elected Official, who has "red" all of the Books that are Listed in Chapter 16?
    1-[_] I would Trust any Person who Actually "red" all such Books.
    2-[_] I would not Trust them, unless they Filled Out and Filed **"The Complete SURVEYS of our VALUES!"** Book 059.
    3-[_] I would only Trust the Person who has Checked the Boxes with Statements that I Agree with in ALL of those Inspired Books.
    4-[_] I would only Trust the Person who has a Good Reputation for being Honest with me, even if he or she is not Honest with other People.
    5-[_] I would only Trust the Person who is Honest with all People.
    6-[_] It is not Practical for People to always be Perfectly Honest. For Example, what will be your Answer if some Child Asks you whether or not you have had Sexual Intercourse with someone before getting Married?
    7-[_] It is none of that Child's Concern, who might Ask all Kinds of Embarrassing Questions like that, which are none of his Business, nor anyone else's Business:

beCause it is a Personal Thing. Therefore, there are no such Private Questions in **"The Complete SURVEYS of our VALUES!"**

8-[_] It is Comforting to Learn that those Surveys are not Concerning our Personal Sins; but, only our RELIGIOUS, Spiritual, Political, Governmental, Sexual, Social, Moral, Economic, Business, Labor, Habitual, and Miscellaneous VALUES, which any Honest Person can Agree or Disagree with. For Example, "Do you Believe in God?"

A-[_] Yes, B-[_] No, C-[_] Cannot Decide.

9-[_] I would Trust the Person who Loves and Obeys the Hebrew God, who Commanded the Children of Israel to go into the Land of Canaan, and Murder every Living Creature, including the Cats and Dogs, and to Dash the Children's Heads against the Stone Walls. †§‡ (See *First Samuel 15:3, KJV*.)

R-[_] No Righteous God would ever Command anyone to Do such an Evil Thing.

S-[_] All of the Saints would have Dashed the Heads of the Children of Canaan against the Stone Walls: so that their Spirits could be Born Again into Israelite Families, which is a Chief Belief of Bashar al Assad of Syria. ‡

T-[_] I would not be Tempted to do any such Evil Thing as Murdering Innocent Children.

U-[_] You do not Understand the Master Plan of the Master Farmer, who is a Man of WAR! (See *Exodus 15:3, KJV*.)

V-[_] The Victims of Capitalism, Communism, Socialism, Fascism, and other Isms have no Use for VIOLENCE. Indeed, they Prefer to Settle all Disputes in Courtrooms with Righteous Judges in Charge.

W-[_] The Warmongering Israelites had to Invent a False God, just to have an Excuse for Murdering the Canaanites, Hittites, Hivites, Jebuzites, Gerguziits, Hutterites, and Mennonites. †§‡§§

X-[_] X-amount of People have been Deceived by the *Holy Bible*, which should be brought to Court: beCause it is an Invention of Lying Red Jews, who cannot be Trusted.

Y-[_] I will not Yield to any such Temptations: because the *Bible* is a Perfect Book, even if there are 200+ Versions of it.

Z-[_] The Zeal of **The Worldwide People's Revolution!®** will make it Possible to Straighten Out this Confusion and Madness.

06-02 [_] It is Obvious that most of the People in **The Divided States of United Lies** are NOT Righteous, or else they would Cheerfully Fill Out and File **"The Complete SURVEYS of our VALUES!"** on the Internet, for everyone to Study, and especially if they are Running for some Political Office: because they have nothing to be Ashamed of. However, Outlaws and Criminals have many Evil Things to HIDE from the Electors, even as Jesus said, who will not come into the Light of Truths, lest their Evil Deeds should be Exposed. (See *John 3:20—21*.)

(The so-called "United States of North America," in Disguise!)

06-03 [_] I Sincerely Believe that if all Moneys were done away with, along with Capitalism, Socialism, Communism, Fascism, and all other Isms, the Saying would come to pass, that: **"SWANGKEENOMIKS Rules the Roost!" (HOW all People can Prosper in a RIIT WAA, and STOP Polluting the Earth with Capitalist TRASH!) By The Worldwide People's Revolution!® Book 039.**

06-04 [_] I am Afraid to Study any such Inspired Books: beCause I cannot Imagine Living without Money, even if it is the CAUSE for almost all of our Major EVILS.

06-05 [_] Well, at least you are Honest about it, which is somewhat like a Confession. Therefore, you might as well make a Full Confession of ALL of our Financial and Dietary Sins, whereby you might Escape from the Capitalist Prison of Lies and Deceptions. ‡

06-06 [_] Will we all have to be Branded with *the Mark of the Beast,* just as *the Book of Revelation* Reveals, just for Rejecting the Truths about a RIGHTEOUS One-World Government? Will we all have to get our RFID (Radio Frequency Identification) Chips Implanted under the Skins of our Right Hands, or under the Skins of our Foreheads, if we do not have Right Hands: beCause of getting them Chopped Off for Stealing Candy Bars in Gross Grocery Stores?

06-07 [_] Why not Yield to the Will of God, who is Obviously NOT the Cruel Hebrew God; but, the Heavenly Father of Jesus Christ, who was a Man of True Love and Great Compassion?

06-08 [_] I much Prefer to Live in the Wilderness with the Bears and Snakes, than to Live with Lying Hypocrites, who Profess to Believe in Jesus Christ, and then Act like Satan and Sons, Incorporated, who can never get Enough Money, who Rob and Cheat other People for Gain. §

06-09 [_] I much Prefer to Order all of those Lying Red Jews into COURT, and have them Prove that they are Worthy to Handle our Money, after Collecting TRILLIONS of Dollars from us by Usury Slavery!

06-10 [_] I have no Idea what Usury Slavery IS. Is that some Major Sin of Lying Red JEWS? Are they not God's Chosen People?

— Chapter 07 —

Loaning Money for Interest

07-01 [_] God's Chosen People would have the Spirit of Fathers Abraham, Isaac, and Jacob, who did not Rob their Poor Naaberz for any Selfish Reasons. In Fact, if you Study *Genesis,* you will Discover that rather than make War, those Saints RE-DUG the Wells that their Enemies Filled in, and not just once nor twice; but, many Times. Therefore, we might well Ask ourselves if the present-day Israelis have the SPIRIT of Israel, whose Name was Changed from Jacob to Israel, which Means: *Man who Prevails with God,* after he Wrestled Naked all Night with Jehovah God, by the Brook called *Penuel,* where the Family of Jacob passed over into the Promised Land, which you can read about in *Genesis 32*.

07-02 [_] *Exodus 22:25—27* reads as follows: *"If you Lend Money to any of my People who are Poor, who are Living beside you, you shall not be to him like an Usurer, who Charges Interest on Loans; neither shall you lay on him any Usury, nor take any Usury from him, nor any Increase: because he is already a Poor Person, who does not need to be more Poorer than he already is by Paying Usury; but, you shall Fear the Supreme Judge, your God, who Loves Justice and Equity. Therefore, if you at all Accept your Naaber'z Clothing as a Pledge to Repay you for something, you shall Deliver that Clothing to him by the Time that the Sunstar goes down: because that is his only Covering. Indeed, it is his Clothing to Protect his Skin. Therefore, without it, wherein shall he Sleep during the Cold Nights? Therefore, it shall come to pass that when he Cries out to me for Justice, that I will Hear his Cry: because I am Gracious and Merciful; and therefore, I will be Forced to Punish you for your Greed. After all, if you Establish a Righteous Government, there will be no Good Excuse for anyone to be so Poor, nor for anyone to be Loaning Money for Usury: because everyone will be Able to Earn as much Money as he might Want, in Exchange for the Stonework that he does for the Construction of Beautiful Planned City States. Yes, that Good Government will simply Mint and Print the Necessary New Money for Hiring whomever is Willing and Able to Learn and Work, in Order to Construct all such City States, each of which will Govern itself According to my Commandments, which are Just and Good for all of you. After all, if you were Extremely Poor, would you Want some Greedy Person Loaning Money to you for Usury, whereby you would be made Poorer than you already are? Absolutely not! Therefore, why would you Want to do such an Evil Thing to your Naaberz? Therefore, do as I say, and Establish a Righteous GovernMint, which does what is Right for all of the People: so that you do not Produce any Criminals among you, who are made into Criminals by Means of the Injustices that are done to them, whereby they become Rebellious People, and even Thieves, Liars, Robbers, and Murderers: because of being Robbed, Deceived, and Cheated."* — The New MAGNIFIED Version (NMV) in Plain English

07-03 [_] O Elected King, if those Exact Words had been in the *GAY King James Version,* this World would have been a much Better Place to Live. Therefore, I like Verse 28, which reads: *"You shall not Revile against the Gods who Govern you, nor Curse any of the Rulers of your People, whom you have Elected to Rule Over you by Popular Votes: because it is Possible and most Practical for People with Different Opinions and Beliefs to Move into New Planned City*

States, whereby they can Live According to their own Elected Laws and Flexible Rules, and thus Live in Peace with Like-minded People, whereby everyone can be Happy with their Elections."
— NMV

07-04 [_] O Elected King, I do Wish to God that all such Inspired Words of Provable Truths were Found in the very GAY *King James Version (KJV),* whereby we could have Avoided all of those Election Deceptions, Political Lies, False Promises, Gang Wars, Gun Violence, Mass Shootings, and all of the EVILS that go on in these Cities of Confusion: beCause of Living with Like-minded People within those **"GLORIOUS Swanky Hotels Castles and Fortresses!" (Beautiful Planned City States for WISE Intelligent Well-Educated People with Common Sense and Good Understanding!) By The Worldwide People's Revolution!®** Book 019.

07-05 [_] Well, those Lying Red Jews would not have Liked that Plan: because, then they would not be Able to Collect TRILLIONS of Dollars for USURY! Indeed, they Especially Love to Collect Usury on so-called "Pay-day Loans," whereby they can Legally Collect as much as 400% Interest on one-day Loans, and from Extremely Poor People, whereby they are Directly Disobeying the Laws of God that he gave to Moses! ‡

07-06 [_] Such Interest Masters should be taken out and Hanged to the nearest Trees, before Morning: because they know full well what they are doing, and it is EVIL. †§‡

07-07 [_] So, is that what you would Want someone to Do to YOU, if they Judged that you might be doing something EVIL? Why not bring the United States Congress to COURT, and Prove to them that they are the Chief Criminals!? And then, if they do not Confess it, and Agree to Establish **"The New RIGHTEOUS One-World Government,"** we can have them Legally HANGED, or Boiled in Used Motor Oil, directly in front of **"The BIG White OUTHOUSE on the Not-so-Biblical Capitol DUNGHILL!"** Yes, they Profess to be True Christians, who have Sworn an Oath to Defend the Citizens against all Enemies, both Foreign and Domestic, which would Naturally Include those Lying Red JEWS, who have Robbed Americans of TRILLIONS of Dollars, which can easily be Proven in a Courtroom with Law and Order! Yes, it should be Proven at: **"The Great Worldwide TELEVISED Court HEARING!" (That Great Meeting of the Most Intelligent Minds!) By The Worldwide People's Revolution!®** Book 041.

07-08 [_] O Elected King, I do Wish to God that your Name were on the Election Ballot, this Year. {See www.Amazon.com for: **"Mark Twain Races for the PRESIDENCY!" (The 2016 Presidential Candidates Desperately Need Some STRONG Undefeatable COMPETITION!) By The Worldwide People's Revolution!®** Book 033.}

07-09 [_] O Elected King, it is too Late to Vote for you: because the Year is Slipping by too Fast, and Election Day will soon be Passed, and your Name will not even be on the Ballot. Therefore, what should we Do about it? Indeed, you are likely to be Dead within another 4 Years: because of being Old and Defeated by our Unbelief. †§‡

07-10 [_] Well, "There is more than one Way to Skin a Cat," as the Old Saying goes; and, in this Case, we can "Skin the Cat" by NOT Voting for anyone, whereby all of those Politicians will go Home with their Tales of Lies tucked between their Legs, you might say. After all, just Imagine how Ashamed they would Feel, if almost no one Voted for them? However, it is also too Late in the Season to Accomplish that — unless some Rich Person should put a Copy of this Inspired Book into every Mailbox in America, along with: **"The New RIGHTEOUS One-World Government!" (HOW to Establish a Righteous One-World Government without Going to WAR!) By The Worldwide People's Revolution!®** Book 056. Yes, that would be a Great Sacrifice; but, it is a Possibility. However, if that Fails, even as it most likely will, there is still another Option, which is called a Non-violent Protest, whereby the Masses of People simply GO TO BED, and STAY IN BED, until the Leaders of all Nations DEMAND: **"The Great Worldwide TELEVISED Court HEARING!"** Yes, that Inspired Book could also be put into those Mailboxes by Amazon.com — that is, IF the Masters at Amazon are Sick and Tired of the EVILS of Capitalism, who would much rather be Living in those **"Beautiful Swanky PALACES!" (A New Concept in Living Habits!) By The Worldwide People's Revolution!®** Book 066.

— Chapter 08 —

Segregation has now become a GOOD Thing!

08-01 [_] I will first give to you the Definition of "Segregation," according to the Dictionary and also According to the *Bible,* which Teaches the Doctrine of Segregation.

> A-[_] the action or state of setting someone or something apart from other people or things or being set apart, for example: *the segregation of pupils with learning difficulties.* In other words, the Pupils with Learning Disabilities need Special Care, just to Teach to them the same Lessons that "Normal" Students might Quickly Learn — such as Swanky "Funetik Ingglish," which a "Normal Student" could Learn within Minutes, and thus be able to Spell any Word in the English Language without the Use of a Dictionary. ‡

> B-[_] the enforced separation of different racial groups in a country, community, or establishment, for example: *an official policy of racial segregation.* In other words, not many Years Ago, in the Divided States of United Lies, the "Black" Children were not Permitted to Attend "White" Schools, which was called "Segregation of the Races." Moreover, many Businesses and even Churches also Practiced Racial Segregation, whereby "Black" People were not Welcome in such Places, which is still the Case in many Churches and Businesses, even if there are no Signs Warning anyone about it. Indeed, it is just Understood that there are "Forbidden Territories" in the Divided States of United Lies.

08-02 [_] So, O Elected King, are you Proposing that we Americans Return to those Bad Old Days, or what?? Would you SEPARATE the Black People from the White People, who are not Actually Black nor White, as in Black and White Paper?

(The so-called "United States of North America," in Disguise!)

08-03 [_] Well, anyone and everyone is Welcome to Check any of the following Boxes with an X, if they Agree with such Statements; and then we will take up the Issue from there.

    A-[_] I am Against Segregation. I do NOT Believe in it.

    B-[_] I Believe in Segregation: beCause the *Scriptures* say, *"Come OUT from among the Wicked Ones, and be you Separated from them, says the Supreme Ruler, and Touch NONE of their Unclean Things; and then I will Receive you, and be a Loving Father unto you; and you shall become my Holy Sons and Purified Daughters."* — Second Corinthians 6:17, NMV.

    C-[_] All such Quotes must be Accepted in CONTEXT with the Remaining Words in the Chapter. Indeed, the Doctrine begins in Verse 14, which reads as follows: *"Be you not Unequally Yoked Together with Unbelievers: because it is Confusion to Plow with an Ox and an Ass Together, or with a Camel and a Donkey: because they are not Matched up Properly. Indeed, what Fellowship does Righteousness have with Unrighteousness? And what Communion does Light have with Darkness, seeing that they are Contrary to one another? Moreover, what Concord is there between Christ and Satan? Or, what Part of an Inheritance does a Believer have with an Unbeliever, who is called an Infidel? Furthermore, what Agreement does the Temple of God have with Idols, which are Abominations, which can neither See, Hear, Smell, Taste, nor Feel anything, being as Dead and Lifeless as a Rock, you might say? Indeed, your Minds and Bodies are the Temple of the Living God, even as God has said: 'I will Live within them, and will Walk and Talk with them, and Remind them of my Commandments; and thus I will be their God, and they shall be my Chosen People: because of becoming Holy, even as I am Holy. Yes, they will Humble themselves by Means of Fasting and Praying, until they Obtain Purified Minds and Holy Bodies, even as those of Innocent Holy Children, whereby I may Live within them. Therefore, come Out from among the Wicked Ones, and be you Separated from them, says the Supreme Ruler, and Touch not their Unclean Things; and then I will Receive you into my Arms of Love and Mercy, and will be a Loving Father unto you, and you shall become my Beloved Sons and Purified Daughters, says the Commanding General of Seven Great Armies of Working Soldiers.' Therefore, having those Promises, dearly Beloved Brothers, let us Cleanse ourselves from all Filthiness of the Flesh and Spirit by Means of Fasting and Praying, even as Moses and Elijah Cleansed themselves, whereby they Shined with the Glory of the Gods, even Perfecting their Holiness in the Fear of Jehovah God, who is the God of the Hebrews, whom we will do Well to Imitate in all Ways, and thus get Rid of those Canaanites."* — NMV †§‡

    D-[_] Damn it! — that is NOT what it says! You have Added LIES to the Word of God, which is ONE Word, which is JESUS, who never said a Word about Fasting nor Praying, much less Fasting until we become HOLY, even as he is HOLY: beCause God does not give a DAMN about Holiness of Mind, Spirit, nor Body — and especially our Bodies, which are the Temples of Gluttony, Drunkenness, Sicknesses, Diseases, and all such Good Things as Lumps, Tumors, Abscesses, Pimples, Boils, and Cancers! Yes, all of the Gods are Covered with Boils from their Heads to their Toes, just as Jobe was! †§‡§§

    E-[_] Educated People do not have to Curse, in order to Express their Honest Opinions.

F-[_] I Fail to Understand what any of that has to do with SEGREGATION?

G-[_] God Knows that you Missed the Message in Verse C. Perhaps your Mind was Blinded by that *"Commanding General of Seven Great Armies of Working Soldiers!"*?

H-[_] I am an Honest Person. I will Speak the Truth, if I am Asked for it.

I-[_] Innocent People already Realize the Need for SEGREGATION Between Righteous People and Wicked People: beCause Light has no Fellowship with Darkness; but, what does that have to do with Separating the RACES?

J-[_] Justice Demands that a Righteous One-World Government must be Established, which Favors the Righteous People, and Assists them to Build those **"GLORIOUS Swanky Hotels Castles and Fortresses,"** even if they are so-called "Atheists": because, if they are Righteous People, who Obey the Laws of Justice and Equity, they are Worthy of our Assistance. Yes, they only have to Agree to Live Moral Righteous Lives. ‡

K-[_] When King Jesus Establishes his Righteous One-World Government, he will Separate the White Peoples from the Black Peoples: because it is not Right that White Peoples should be Ruling Over Black Peoples, nor that Black Peoples should be Ruling Over White Peoples. †§‡

L-[_] Lots of Laughs! King Jesus will Cause all Good Souls to be Born in White Bodies, and all Bad Souls to be Born in Black Bodies, according to their Wickedness, whereby the most Wicked ones will be Born in the Blackest Bodies. †§‡

M-[_] Monkeys will Enter into the Kingdom of God before People like you. †§‡

N-[_] *"Not everyone who says unto me, 'Lord, Lord,' shall Enter into the Kingdom of God, which is coming from Heaven to the Renewed Earth; but, he who does the Will of my Father, who Lives in the Sky."* — NMV of Matthew 7:21.

O-[_] Are there no OPTIONS? How about letting the People Separate themselves as they Want to, whereby they have True Freedom? Indeed, if some White People Want to Live with some Black People, who do not Object to it, let them. Likewise, if some Black People Want to Live with some White People, who do not Object to it, let them. ‡

P-[_] I Choose to Live with Like-minded People, only.

Q-[_] The Great Question is this, **"Will God be Pleased with us, if we Mongrelize ourselves by Mixing as many Races Together as Possible?"**

R-[_] I Choose to Live with Righteous People, ONLY. Therefore, if we Discover some Wicked Person among us, we will simply Cast him or her OUT of our Swanky Fortress.

S-[_] I Choose to Separate myself from all People, and Live in the Bob Marshal Wilderness with the Snakes and Bears: because you People are CRAZY! †§‡

(The so-called "United States of North America," in Disguise!)

T-[_] I Like BIG Long Tally Whackers. Therefore, I Choose to Live with similar People.

U-[_] I Understand that each Person should be Free to Choose the Kind of People that he or she Likes Best. Otherwise, it would not be True Freedom.

V-[_] The Victims of Segregation will be Deprived of the Great Diversities of People whom God has Created for us to Richly Enjoy.

W-[_] I Like all Peoples in the World; but, that does not Mean that I should have to Live in the same House with them, nor even within the same Planned City State. However, if someone Chooses to Live in a Mongrelized City of Confusion, that Person should have the Freedom to do so, and it will not Bother me.

X-[_] X-amount of People will just Naturally Separate themselves into Similar Colors, even as a large Field with Diverse Colors of Cattle just Naturally Separate themselves with their own Kind. For Example, if you put 20 Black Cattle in a large Field with 20 White Cattle, they will just Naturally Separate themselves from one another by their Colors. Likewise, if you put a certain Breed of Sheeps or Goats in the same Field with another Breed, they will soon Separate themselves — that is, IF there is a Distinct Difference between them, even as Deers will Separate themselves from Antelopes and Mountain Goats. ‡

Y-[_] That might have been Good during Yesteryears; but, now we are Educated, and Understand that God has made of ONE BLOOD all Nations of Men for the Purpose of Living on all of the Surface of the Earth, and has Determined the Times and Events, which were Appointed Long Ago, including the Bounds of their Habitations: so that they might Seek the Creator, if per Chance they might Feel for him, and thus Find him, even though he is not Far Away from every one of us: because, in him we Live, and Move, and have our Being; even as certain ones among your Poets have also said: because we are also his Offsprings. Forasmuch then as we are the Offsprings of Gods, we ought not to Think that the Godhead is like Gold, Silver, nor Stones, nor Graven by the Arts of Men, according to their Devices. (See *Acts 17:26—29*.)

Z-[_] You are Zealous to Believe all such Biblical Nonsense, which was written without Good Understanding. After all, there are many Types of Blood among People, even as there are many Kinds and Colors: because not all Peoples have the same Natures: because many of them were Transported here from other Worlds of the same Order as this World. Yes, they were Living here for hundreds and thousands — yes, even Millions of Years — before Jehovah God formed the Body of Adam from the Elements of the Ground, who was the First White Man on the Earth, which you would Understand, if you had Studied: **"In thu Beeginingz uv Thingz!" (Thu Kreeaashun Stooree frum thu Beegining!) By The Worldwide People's Revolution!® Book 025.**

08-04 [_] I am Greatly Confused by the FACTS. Please do not Confuse us with any more Facts. It is Okay to Crossbreed Black People with Blond People, whereby the Children are Born with Red Hairs and Freckles, which they all LOVE: beCause they are CUTE. Yes, they are Especially Cute when they are getting Teased by their Fellow Students in **"The Public School of**

IGNERUNT FQLZ!" (HOW we have been GRAATLEE DISEEVD!) By The Worldwide People's Revolution!® Book 024. †§‡§§

08-05 [_] Satan would have us to Believe that it is a Good Thing for us to Crossbreed the Races; but, God Forbids it: beCause it is like Crossbreeding Peacocks with Chickens, whereby the Beauty of the Peacocks is Destroyed. Indeed, God much Prefers that each Race and Breed should keep itself as Pure as Possible: beCause only the Most Pure Races will have any Inheritance in the Holy Kingdom of the Gods. Moreover, there are certain *Scriptures* to Support this Doctrine, which you can Discover in *Ezra 10* and *Nehemiah 13—14,* and Related *Scriptures,* which few People Study; and while you are Studying those *Scriptures,* you should Understand that it was a Major SIN that the Israelites Committed, whereby they Slew all of those Foreign Wives and their Children, just to Prevent the Wrath of Jehovah God from Destroying all of them. ‡

08-06 [_] It is my Honest Belief that we may Marry anyone who Loves us, in spite of their Color, Race, Creed, Religion, Sexual Orientation, Financial Status, or whatever: because God does not Love a Cast System, such as they have in India. †§‡

08-07 [_] No one should be Forced to Live with People that he or she does not Love: because that could make them Unhappy, and thus Unhealthy, which would Defeat the very Notion of True Freedom and the Pursuit of Happiness, which Begins with Good Health.

08-08 [_] Well, if we Build those **"GLORIOUS Swanky Hotels Castles and Fortresses,"** it will not be Difficult to Separate all of the People with Like-minded People, whereby they might all be Happy with each other, and also Trade with whomever they Trust, even if they are of other Races, Nations, Colors and Kinds, which will be their Decisions to make. ‡

08-09 [_] Will certain Fortresses not be Teaching HATE for the People within other Fortresses of Contrary Beliefs and/or Colors?

08-10 [_] Well, if they do, they can be Shunned. However, it is Better to put them to Open Shame at some Great Meeting of the Most Intelligent Minds, where they will be Welcome to Defend their Beliefs by Means of Reason and Logic, even if they are Members of the Klu Klux Klamz.

— Chapter 09 —

Equal Opportunities must be Guaranteed!

09-01 [_] The Chief Reason for Establishing **"The New RIGHTEOUS One-World Government"** is to Assure everyone in the World of Equal Opportunities, in as much as it is Possible, even if it is a bit Impractical: beCause of several Reasons. For Example, it is not very Practical to Build a Complex Railroad System to the Remote Jungle Tribes of Africa, whereby

Mountains of Rocks can be Transported to them, if they are Contented to Live in Mud Huts. However, just to Treat them Justly, if there are enough of them in some Tribe to Build such a Fortress, they should be Helped to do it, even if they must Move to a Better Location, which might be as little as 200 to 400 Miles away, depending on the Terrain. Indeed, Swamps are not Ideal Places to begin Building any such Fortresses. Geologists must Study all such Situations, and give their Honest Opinions.

09-02 [_] I would say that only Ideal Places in Africa should be Developed with Swanky Fortresses: because there are Vast Territories that are Ideal for Wild Animals, who should be left alone, and perhaps Supplied with Reliable Sources of Foods and Water, as if we were Good Stewards. ‡

09-03 [_] Well, it is for Sure that all Civilized Societies can be Assisted to Prosper Properly, if they are Interested in Living in **"Beautiful Swanky PALACES!" (A New Concept in Living Habits!) By The Worldwide People's Revolution!®** Book 066.

09-04 [_] O Elected King, will **"The New RIGHTEOUS One-World Government"** take the Beautiful Marble away from the Italians, for Example, and give it to those Lazy Africans, who would not even know HOW to Use it? †§‡

09-05 [_] Well, I am Sure that the Italians have lots of Marble that they would not Object to Sharing with Africans, if they have none. Otherwise, the United States of America has lots of Marble and Granite, which it will be Happy to Share with Poor African Nations, or any other Poor Nations. Indeed, most Nations will Discover Marble and Granite Rocks to Share with other Nations, in Exchange for some of their Marbles and Granites, Fruits, Nuts, or whatever they have to Share. After all, there are Literally hundreds of thousands of Mountains of Rocks in this World of Wonders, which we can Use Wisely for Building **"The Environmentalists' Paradise!" (HOW almost Everyone could be Living in a Beautiful Manmade Paradise!) By The Worldwide People's Revolution!®** Book 035.

09-06 [_] So, O Elected King, what will Happen if those Nations do not Cooperate with you, and Refuse to go to Work?

09-07 [_] Well, they will be Welcome to Present their most Reasonable Arguments at: **"The Great Worldwide TELEVISED Court HEARING,"** which will not be Fencing Out Dissidents nor Dissenters: beCause, like the "Conversations" within all of my Inspired Books, their Arguments will be Welcome. However, I now give to all Dissenters Fair WARNING that **"The Swanky Sword of Divine Truths"** may easily Remove their Heads, and put them to Open Shame. Therefore, it is Wise of them to Study all of my Inspired Books, Carefully, before making Fools of themselves.

09-08 [_] O Elected King, what if you should Accidentally DIE between now and then — WHO would take up that Sword of Truths, whereby the Potential Enemies might be put into Silence?

09-09 [_] Well, if you Seek for a Wise Man, who has the Gift of the Holy Spirit, who will Remind him of the Right Answers, I am Sure that you will Discover those Answers. Otherwise, you will need to be Wise, and Assign Segments or Chapters of the Books to People with Good Minds, who might Remember the Words, and thus Present the Best Answers.

09-10 [_] O Elected King, suppose Important Questions are brought up, which your Inspired Books do not Address — HOW will we Answer such Questions?

— Chapter 10 —

The Tough Questions

10-01 [_] Any Intelligent Person can begin Asking Tough Questions, which no one on the Earth can Rightly Answer: beCause of getting into Scientific Subjects, and Vain Things that Wise People should not be Concerned with. For Example, How should we Build a Spaceship that Travels Faster than Light: so that we can Visit other Worlds?

10-02 [_] First of all, we need to Learn WHY we were Born HERE, instead of being Born in those other Worlds. After all, if God Wanted us to be Exploring other Worlds, he could have Caused our Spirits to be Born in Bodies over there, instead of here. Therefore, there is no Need for any such Spaceships.

10-03 [_] O King, I would say that the Federal Government of the United States already knows HOW to Build Flying Saucers and other Spacecraft that they do not tell us about. After all, they have Sneaky Things going on in Area 51, in Nevada. Therefore, it would be Difficult to say what all the Government knows.

10-04 [_] Well, whatever Information they have Hidden from us Tax Slaves, we can Disclose it at: **"The Great Worldwide TELEVISED Court HEARING!" (That Great Meeting of the Most Intelligent Minds!) By The Worldwide People's Revolution!®** Book 041.

10-05 [_] So, O King, would we Reveal all of our Top Secrets to the Russians and Chinese Peoples? Would we give the Blueprints for the Intercontinental Ballistic Missiles to the North Koreans and Cubans?

10-06 [_] Well, after their Representatives come to that Great Meeting of the most Intelligent Minds, and Contribute their Objections to Living in **"Beautiful Swanky PALACES,"** we might Consider Entrusting them with all such Blueprints, seeing that they did not Drop any Atomic Bombs on any Enemies, nor even any Firebombs. For Example, the United States Firebombed no less than 10,000 Cities during World War 2, including Dresden, Germany, whereby they Murdered more than 100,000 Innocent People, most of whom were Women and Children, who were Incinerated in Devouring FIRE, which was "a True Christian Act," you might say; but, I would call it an Act of the Synagogue of Satan, for which the Federal Government of the Divided States of United Lies should Apologize to the Germans, who actually had Justified

Reasons for going to War, which can be, should be, and must be Proven in a Courtroom! Likewise, it could be that the North Koreans also have Justified Reasons for being the Way they are, which they can Present to the World at that Great Meeting, along with the Palestinians and other so-called "Enemies," including ISIS, the Taliban, and whomever Hates our Guts, who likely have Reasons for it, which we all Need to Learn: beCause it might Help us to Understand them, and also Answer their Important Questions, if they can Present them in such a Way that they are Understandable. After all, there is the Language Barrier to get around, whereby just one Word in the English Language might have a hundred Different Definitions! Therefore, when a Translator is saying something that is very Sarcastic, it is Extremely easy to get it Misunderstood or Mistranslated. Therefore, we must Learn to be very Patient with other People, and give to them the Benefit of the Doubt, and Trust that they are Sincere.

10-07 [_] O King, do you Sincerely Believe that the North Korean Government would Televise that entire Meeting of the Minds to ALL of the People in North Korean, and without adding any of their Propagandist LIES?

10-08 [_] Well, you might also Turn it Around, and Ask whether or not you Sincerely Believe that you have Heard ALL Sides of the Issues from your own Anti-Christ False Cover-up Federal Government and Red Jew News Media? Chances are that you have NOT: beCause Capitalism also has its own Agenda. Therefore, it is very Important to get Honest Translators, who are Qualified to Translate all of the Words Correctly, even if they are Sarcastic, which might Prove to be Difficult. Whatever the Case, LOVE will Overcome a Multitude of Sins, if we Use it.

10-09 [_] O King, if you do not know the Answer to some Question, you can always say: "Well that Question will be Answered at **'The Great Worldwide TELEVISED Court HEARING,'"** which it may be, or may not be! Indeed, HOW will we Discover enough TIME to Answer MILLIONS of Questions?

10-10 [_] Well, most of our Questions are likely already Answered in Good Books, if those Questions are concerning Good Living. Therefore, it is Important that Authors from around the World should be Prepared to Present their Best Answers, which can be Presented in the **"FREEDUM uv SPEECH!" (U Speshoul Maguzeen uv Onust Upinyunz!) By The Worldwide People's Revolution!®** Book 030-0002—9999. Yes, that Magazine of Opinions will be Full of Questions and Answers, all of which will be Graded for their Importance: so as to not Waste too much Time with Foolish Questions and Ridiculous Answers.

— Chapter 11 —

Gun Control without Guns!

11-01 [_] If you have Watched News Reports on TV about Gun Violence throughout the World — such as the Radical Muslim Massacre in Orlando, Florida, in June of 2016, whereby Omar Mateen Murdered 49 People at the Pulse Nightclub — you might Wonder just HOW any such Crimes could be Prevented? After all, some of the Security Guards had Weapons; but, they were apparently Useless for Defending the People in that Nightclub.

11-02 [_] O Elected King, when we Build those **"GLORIOUS Swanky Hotels Castles and Fortresses,"** it will be Impossible for any such Gun-toting Criminals to get into them: because everyone will have to be Thoroughly Searched for any Weapons before being Allowed to Enter into them. Indeed, most of those Fortresses will Require that all Visitors go into Private Shower Rooms, Remove their Clothing, put the Clothing into a Locked Box, take a Shower, and put on Identity Clothing — such as Special Robes, whereby they can be Recognized as Visitors; and then Special Guards will be Assigned to Guard them and the People within the Fortress, who will Act as Policemen; but, without any Weapons: because they will be Trained for Hand-to-Hand Combat, whereby they will be able to Defend themselves, who will Work in Pairs as Teams of Guards, who will also have Emergency Backup Teams, if they are Needed, who may have Weapons, being One-World Government Guards. Otherwise, if those Visitors appear to be Harmless and Cooperative, they may be Escorted by Tour Guides at the Hotels, who will be able to Call for Help, if they need it. After all, there will be Busloads of Old People coming from Various Countries to take Grand Tours, who will not need to be Guarded very Closely, who may have already Filled Out and Filed **"The Complete SURVEYS of our VALUES,"** whereby they can be Trusted. Nevertheless, Security Cameras will still be Watching them and everyone else at most large Swanky Fortresses: because it will be Assumed that no one can be Fully Trusted — at least until all such Hate Crimes have Ceased for several Years, which they will eventually do: because People who are Moderately Rich, and Living in **"Beautiful Swanky PALACES,"** have no Desire to Murder other People. Moreover, Minority Groups of People — such as the LGBTQ Communities — will be Extra Cautious when letting Visitors come into their Fortresses, who may even have to pass Lie Detector Tests, and be Vetted by Professional People, if they are Suspicious-looking, or have a History of being Violent, who may even be Handcuffed to a Security Guard, just to Discover whether or not he is Cooperative and Flexible. †§‡

11-03 [_] Well, some of those Swanky Fortresses will Require that all Visitors without Proper Credentials will have to Fast for 40 Days, just to be Permitted within their Cities: beCause of not Wanting any Potential Criminals within their Cities of Holy People, which 40 Days will be used Wisely for Teaching Visitors whatever the Fortified People Believe. After all, no one will have to Visit any such Cities, nor do any Fasting at all. However, when they get to See their Holy Faces, most People will just Naturally fall in Love with them; and therefore, they will Want to get into those Cities to Discover Friends and Lovers, even if they must Fast for 40 Days or more. {See www.Amazon.com for: **"HOW to Become a HOLY Man!"** (40 Good Reasons WHY People Should FAST and PRAY!) By The Worldwide People's Revolution!® Book 045.}

11-04 [_] So, O Elected King, it Sounds as if there will be many Different Plans for Screening OUT any Potential Criminals from those **"GLORIOUS Swanky Hotels Castles and Fortresses!"** Indeed, some of them will likely be Strip-Searching the Visitors, just to Discover their Nakedness, and to Secretly Photograph them with Hidden Cameras while they are taking Showers. In Fact, I would not be Surprised to Learn that some Young People will be getting Raped by the Guards. †§‡

11-05 [_] Well, if any such Evil Things Happen, it will not be by the Permission of **"The New RIGHTEOUS One-World Government!"** Indeed, it is Bound to Happen at Low Class Swanky Fortresses, which have Low Moral Standards — such as the SIXTH and SEVENTH Swanky Fortresses, where Marijuana, Booze, and Prostitution are Legal, as well as other Drugs, which Righteous People will Naturally AVOID. Therefore, I Suggest that if you are Worried about it, to stay away from such Fortresses, or go in Teams, and be Sure to Read all of the Warning Signs, and Obey all of the Rules: so that you do not end up in some Jail, where other Prisoners might Rape you or Mistreat you, which is a Possibility, even if it is very Unlikely: because all such Jails will be Monitored 24/7 by **"The New RIGHTEOUS One-World Government!"**

11-06 [_] So, O King, suppose some Criminal like Omar Mateen somehow Manages to get into a Swanky Fortress, and Steals a Sharp Butcher Knife, and Terrorizes the People in that Fortress with the Knife — what shall be his Punishment when he is Caught?

11-07 [_] Well, if he has not Committed Suicide with the Knife, he will Wish that he had: because his Punishment will be SEVERE and most likely Unusual. For Example, he may be Chopped into little Pieces, beginning with his Toes and Fingers, one at a Time, and one Joint at a Time: so that he can Experience PAINS, and thus never Do such an Evil Thing again, when he is Born in some Lower Order of Worlds with other Evil Spirits. †§‡

11-08 [_] O Elected King, if you were in Charge of **"The New RIGHTEOUS One-World Government,"** would you Actually ALLOW such Cruel Punishments to take Place?

11-09 [_] Well, if the Murderer has been Caught in the Act, and Pleads Guilty to the Crimes that he is Accused of, I would say that his Confessions and Punishments should be Televised to the whole World, just to WARN other Would-be Murderers to Think Twice before Committing any such Crimes against Innocent People within Swanky Fortresses, whereby all such Crimes would no doubt Quickly CEASE — at least within the Fortresses! Moreover, it would all be According to the Elected Laws of each Swanky Fortress: beCause the New Righteous One-World Government would not be Punishing anyone Outside of their Jurisdiction, which would be concerned with whatever goes on in: **"The Great World TEMPLE of PEACE,"** in Jerusalem, which might also have some very Strict Laws to Obey. For Example, if some Man Rapes a Woman in that Temple, he will likely be Castrated for it, Publically, on TV, in Order to Set a Good Example of Disobedient Rapists. After all, if he is that Horny, he should Visit some nearby Hotel that has Prostitutes for Rent, who do not Object to being Raped, who may even Love it. Indeed, you will be Able to get anything you Want at Alice's Restaurant, as they say, including HIV-AIDS and 200+ other Sexually-Transmitted Diseases, and it will not bother me: because it will all be Legal and Biblical. Remember how Judah had Sex with his own Daughter-in-law, whom he Presumed was a Prostitute. (See *Genesis 38*.)

11-10 [_] O Elected King, there seems to be a certain Order to the Madness that you Propose, whereby almost everything is Legal, just as long as it is done with Like-minded People, and not within Cities that Forbid all such Things. For Example, if someone Wants to get Drunk and have Sex with a Painted Skunk, he may do so, Legally, at a Seventh Swanky Fortress. Therefore, Crimes are likely to Increase, rather than Decrease: because the Prodigal Sons of the World will be Free to come and go as they Please. †§‡

— Chapter 12 —

A Sure Cure for Sins

12-01 [_] If you have ever Overeaten on Greasy Pizzas, Cakes and Iced-creams, Pies and Iced-creams, Candy Bars, or even Rancid Corn Chips, whereby you were made Sick by it all, you most likely Lost your Appetite for such Things, and might have even Promised yourself to never do it again. Indeed, some Sensitive People have Experienced such Sicknesses from Eating such Things, and made Resolutions to never Eat them again, which can also be the Case for certain People who Experiment with Unlawful Sex, whereby they Contract certain Diseases, whereby they Swear Off of it Forever: beCause of the Bad Experiences. Indeed, if you had just been in a very Bad Car Accident, and nearly Lost your Life, and laid around in some Hospital for 6 Months or more while Recovering from it, it is Doubtful that you would be Interested in getting into another Car with a Drunken Fool, who Drives at 100 MpH, while talking on the Telephone with some Silly Painted Skunk.

12-02 [_] O King, are you Suggesting that the Right Way to Stop Sinning is to go to Extremes — such as Overeating on Pies and Iced-creams, which form very Bad Acids in the Bowels, which can make a Person Vomit?

12-03 [_] Well, without the Opportunity to do such Things: beCause of being Restricted by some Tyrannical Dominating Government to a Limited Amount of such Foods, one might not Learn just how BAD such Foods are. But, with "Freedom" comes "Opportunities to Sin," which can be very Beneficial for Changing People's Minds, and even much more Effective than a Good Sermon, which all such People might even Ignore, or just go to Sleep in the middle of it. Therefore, Sicknesses and Diseases often have Good Side Effects, even as those Car Accidents have also Changed People's Minds about the Goodness of all such Cars, which Humanity could Live Happily without, if they Lived in those **"GLORIOUS Swanky Hotels Castles and Fortresses,"** which are Designed for True Prosperity, where it is Impossible to get into a Car Accident: beCause there are NO Cars within them. Indeed, they use Electric Elevators, Escalators, and Electric Trains in Underground Tunnels with Beautiful Walls that are Faced with Marble, Granite, or Permanent Ceramic Tiles with Colorful Murals Painted on them. After all, no Honest Person has any Need nor Desire for Breathing the Stinking Exhaust that comes Out of Automobiles and other Noisy Polluting Vehicles. Therefore, all such Honest People will Choose to Live in those Beautiful Planned City States for WISE Intelligent Well-Educated People with

(The so-called "United States of North America," in Disguise!)

Common Sense and Good Understanding, who also Know that they will have to give an Account to God for HOW they have Treated or Mistreated his Good Earth, which is our one and only Eternal Home.

12-04 [_] O Elected King, are you Serious? I have always Believed that I will go to Heaven when I Die, and be RID of this World Forever! Therefore, is that not True?

12-05 [_] Well, Jesus clearly said to Nicodemus, *"No Man has Ascended up to Heaven, except for the Son of a Man of Holiness, who is now in a Heavenly Condition, while you are in a Hellish Condition." — NMV of John 3:13.*

12-06 [_] So, O King, if you and Jesus are Correct, that the Meek People will Inherit the Earth, and that the Kingdom or Government of God will come to the Earth, and that the Will of God will be Done on the Earth, even as it is now Done in Heavenly Places, it Means that I have been Believing a FALSE so-called "Christian" Religion, which has Inspired many People to Mistreat the Earth, and Abuse it for their own Gain, whereby they will be brought into Judgment for it. Yes, many People who seem to be Foremost and Important in this World, are very likely to be the Last to Enter into the Government of our God, who is All that is GOOD; and there is nothing GOOD about those Stinking Noisy Gasoline-powered Vehicles, which are Abominations in the Nostrils of the Gods, who Surely HATE all such Things, and so should we: beCause we can Raise our Standard of Living by several Times, just by Building those **"GLORIOUS Swanky Hotels Castles and Fortresses!"** Therefore, we Tax Slaves, Interest Slaves, Insurance Slaves, Drug Slaves, and Work Slaves must DEMAND: **"The Great Worldwide TELEVISED Court HEARING,"** whereby the Masses of People can Learn the Truth about all such Important Subjects, BEFORE the Oceans RISE UP by 40 Feet, and bring us to RUIN! ‡

12-07 [_] Well, my Friend, you Certainly have the Correct Attitude toward all of those Things, and I Pray to God that you and many other People have the GUTS to Do whatever is Necessary to bring about that Great Meeting of the Most Intelligent Minds, whereby our Massive Problems can be Solved, even if a few Lying Red Jews do not Like it. After all, they will get over it when they also Move into their own **"Beautiful Swanky PALACES!" (A New Concept in Living Habits!) By The Worldwide People's Revolution!® Book 066.**

12-08 [_] O Elected King, rather than be Humiliated by some Car Accident, or even by Overeating on some Greasy Pies with Iced-creams, I Choose to Humble myself by Means of Fasting and Praying, whereby I might Smell Out the Truth about our Pollution, and thus come to the same Happy Conclusion that you have come to, which is to Build those **"GLORIOUS Swanky Hotels Castles and Fortresses,"** which will Solve more than 5,000 Massive and Minor Problems at the same Time, which nothing else on the Earth could ever Do, short of the Elimination of Humanity by some Natural Disaster — such as Yellowstone National Park EXPLODING, whereby the Temperature of the Earth will Drop Down to minus 40 below Zero, Fahrenheit, which will get the Attention of those Foolish People, who are not Prepared for all such EVIL Things, who will be taken by Surprise, and who will Naturally DIE from it: beCause of not having a 7-year Supply of Foods and Fresh Water within Swanky Fortresses. Yes, they might Mock at what I say, Today; but, behold, when their Judgment Day comes, they will be Wishing to God that they had Listened to People like me, and Joined those **"Seven Great Armies of Working Soldiers,"** and gone to WORK! ‡

12-09 [_] Well, it is always Wisest to be Prepared for the Worst Conditions, even if such Conditions never come: beCause it is no Great Loss to have a Good Reliable Food and Water Supply, which could Save your Life, and perhaps many Lives, just for a little Work. Indeed, you can read about Great Famines throughout the *Bible,* beginning during the Days of Adam. (See *The Pearl of Great Price.*)

12-10 [_] O Elected King, if you were in Charge of Things on this Earth, every Family would soon have a 7-year Supply of Foods and Fresh Water, as well as Secure Stone Dome Home Complexes, which could Survive that -40 °F Weather for Years: beCause of the THICKNESS of the Solid Stone Walls and Roofs, which might have 20 feet of Dirt on Top of them, having 3 feet of Topsoil on Top for the Gardens, Vineyards, and Orchards, which would be Patiently Waiting for the Return of Normal Weather. Yes, all such Stone Dome Homes should be fixed to be Sealed Tight from any Gases from such Volcanoes, Enemy Attacks, Gas Leaks, or whatever: beCause neither People nor the Environment can be Trusted. However, your Sure Cure for Sins has left Out the Main Remedy, which is the Saving Grace of Jesus Christ, who Wants everyone to REPENT, According to the LAW of Repentance, which is Revealed in: **"The Proper RULES for FASTING!" (The Complete Instruction Manual for True Repentance!) By The Worldwide People's Revolution!® Book 046.**

— Chapter 13 —

Happy Black People

13-01 [_] Every Educated Person in America knows that African-Americans were Used and Abused as Slaves of one Kind or another ever since the Red Jews brought them to the Americas, and Sold them as Slaves. Indeed, the Vast Majority of them are still SLAVES, even if they Imagine that they are Free: beCause they are Tax Slaves, Interest Slaves, Insurance Slaves, Drug Slaves, Sex Slaves, and Work Slaves in one Form or another, even as almost all White People are: beCause they have no Way around it, being Born into it: beCause it is the Way that those Lying Red Jews have Arranged it. However, one could Argue that all Americans are Free with a Capital F, when Compared with the Slavery of the 1800's, which is just another Self-deception: beCause, in Order to be Truly Free with a Capital F, one would have to be Free from all Debts, Worries, Fears, Heartaches, Sicknesses, Diseases, Headaches, Legaches, Pains, and Sufferings! Yes, one would have to be Free from Gun Violence, Drug Addictions, Medical Doctors, Insurance Bills, Property Taxes, Driver's Licenses, Income Taxes, and all such EVIL Things, which no Righteous Government has any Use for: beCause everyone within that Good Government is Healthy, Wealthy, and WISE. Yes, the Children are Born FREE in all Ways, whereby they do not Suffer with Sicknesses, Diseases, Unemployment, Underemployment, Poverty, Crimes, Depressions, Recessions, Bankruptcies, Bouncing Checks, and Endless BILLS to Pay. Yes, the Telephone would be FREE, along with the Large Flat-screen TV, Surround Sound Music, and Countless Tools to Work with: beCause all such Things, including the Beautiful Stone Dome Home Complexes, would Belong to that New RIGHTEOUS One-World

Government, which would make Sure that everything is made to Endure the Test of Time: so that no one is made into a Slave by it.

13-02 [_] For Example, many Years ago, when I was Uneducated, I Bought a brand new Maytag Washing Machine for 1,100$, which naturally came with a Yearly "Service Agreement," which was like Insurance, which was a Necessity: beCause, some of the Parts might Cost 200 to 400 dollars, or more — such as the Electronics, which made all of those Buttons and Switches Work. However, I Calculated that if the Machine endured for 10 Years without any Repairs, that would Add up to no less than 2,400$, even if the Price of the Service Agreement did not Change, which I Judged that it would: beCause that is **"The Nature of CAPITALISM!" (A List of the EVILS of CAPITALISM!) By The Worldwide People's Revolution!®** Book 038. Therefore, I Declined to get the "Service Agreement," and took a Chance that the Washing Machine would Endure for at least 6 Years. After all, it was a Famous Brand Name, which had a Reputation for being a Good American-made Machine. However, after using it for just one Month, it Broke Down, and Required some Serviceman to Repair it. Therefore, we loaded it back into the Pickup Truck, and Drove it 55 Miles to "Sneers and Robuck" for Repairs, which Required 3 Months to get it "Fixed." Meanwhile, it was a Hot Sweaty Summer, which Required that our Clothes should be Washed, Daily: beCause of Working Hard with Heavy Rocks. Therefore, we could not Afford to run 7 Miles to the nearest small Town, just to Wash the Clothes. Therefore, rather than Waste any Money on it, I Decided, WISELY, to Buy another similar Maytag Washing Machine at the same Store, and get a "Service Agreement" for it, which we did; and behold, within a Month or so, it also Broke Down, which Inspired me to Telephone the Serviceman to get it Repaired, which he did for "free," at no extra Cost: beCause it was Covered by the Service Agreement, which was 239.99$ per Year — at least that Year.

13-03 [_] Now, the Parts that he Replaced Costed no less than 500$: because the first Part that he Ordered and Installed, 2 Days later, did not Fix the Problem. Therefore, he Ordered more Parts, and finally got it Fixed, which stayed Fixed for almost 2 Months, and then Broke Down again. However, by that Time, the first Machine was Repaired, and we picked it up for "free": because they did not Notice that it was the other Machine that had the "Service Agreement," and we just Assumed that they were doing us "Good": because of Buying 2 similar Machines, and the Service Agreement. Whatever the Case, they were Happy, and so were we, except for being about 2,500$ Poorer! Nevertheless, with some added Laundry Soap, we did have Clean Clothes for a few Months, when both Machines Broke Down again, within a Week or so of each other; and the Servicemen came and Repaired them for "free." Meanwhile, Sneers and Robuttocks Discovered that we Owed them 269.99$ for the other Service Agreement, and thus sent to us several Duplicate Bills to Pay, as if we had a half-dozen Washing Machines. Indeed, they were probably Hoping that some Secretary would not Notice the Duplicate Bills, and thus Pay all of them; but, after a few Telephone Calls, we got it Straightened Out, for "free" — that is, after waiting on the Telephone Line for as much as 40 Minutes, in order to get in Contact with a Real Person, while going through the "Press 1," or "Press 2" Buttons, etc., etc. They never did Offer to Reimburse us for Wasting any Time on the Telephone, even as the Friendly Bankers do not Reimburse anyone for Waiting in Long Lines on Payday, just to Cash Checks. Nevertheless, being "free," it is no Big Problem: beCause our Time is of no Value at all. In Fact, my Brother Vern and I put in 30 Years of HARD Work on our Farm, and Lost it all — that is, all but 50,000$ Cash, after Investing no less than 300,000$, PLUS the 30 Years of Slave Labor, whereby we Moved MILLIONS of Pounds by our Hands, in Order to Build our Rock Houses,

100,000-gallon Cistern, All-Mineral Organic Garden, Spring Water House, Tool House, Goat House, and several other Concrete and Rock Buildings — all of which was Traded for a single ROOF on our Retirement Home, which does not even Belong to us, even as I have Explained in other Books — Thanks to those Lying Red Jew Banksters, who Assured us that our Property was Worth at least 2 Million Dollars! However, when the "Great Recession" Struck, we were left with almost nothing, while Millions of other Americans were left with less than nothing, and in Debt to those Greedy Selfish Red Jew Bankers! ‡

13-04 [_] O Elected King, if your Inspired Books Sell BILLIONS of Copies, you and your Brother will be Well Compensated for all of your Efforts, Investments, and Sacrifices. Therefore, you have nothing much to Complain about; but, those Millions of People who have no Books to Sell, nor anything else to Sell, are Royally SCREWED, as they say: beCause, if you do not become the Elected King of **"The New RIGHTEOUS One-World Government,"** they will never be Compensated. ‡

13-05 [_] Well, that is all the more Reason WHY we Tax Slaves, Interest Slaves, Insurance Slaves, Drug Slaves, Sex Slaves, and Work Slaves must DEMAND **"The Great Worldwide TELEVISED Court HEARING,"** just to get JUSTICE with a Capital J. Otherwise, there will be NO Justice, Worldwide.

13-06 [_] O Elected King, I Promise to Say and Do everything within my Power to make Sure that your Inspired Literature is Spread Out all around the World: beCause it is the ONE and ONLY Way that the Masses of People, and especially the Black People, will get some Justice! Yes, those Black People may now Prove that they are Worthy of those **"Beautiful Swanky PALACES!" (A New Concept in Living Habits!) By The Worldwide People's Revolution!®** Book 066.

13-07 [_] Well, I certainly Appreciate your Help, which will be most Effective if you can SELL the Books, whereby you can Keep 90% of the Net Profits, which will also Encourage you to Sell more of them, which will also Encourage other People to Sell them, who can eventually Set Up Book Displays on the Streets, after getting Permission from your Local City Government: beCause of having "Freedom of Speech and of the Press," according to the Constitution. However, do not be Disappointed if you cannot Obtain Permission from certain City Governments: beCause they do not ALL have Freedom of Speech, nor of the Press: because that is just another American LIE, which is the Primary Reason that I call it **"The Divided States of United Lies!" (The so-called "United States of North America," in Disguise!) By The Worldwide People's Revolution!®** Book 058.

13-08 [_] So, O Elected King, which Book should we Attempt to Sell FIRST?

13-09 [_] Well, I Prefer **"The New RIGHTEOUS One-World Government!" (HOW to Establish a Righteous One-World Government without Going to WAR!) By The Worldwide People's Revolution!®** Book 056. After all, it is small and easy to read during just one Day, and does not Cost too much for Poor People to Afford, who will be the Backbone of this entire Revolution, which will be Peaceful and Enlightening to the Minds of whomever gets Involved. Indeed, even those Lying Red Jews will Learn to Love it with a Capital L.

13-10 [_] Well, O King, I must Confess that it is a Worthy Experiment, except that I do not have much Hope in Americans Seeing the Light, as Hank Williams might say: beCause they are some of the most Proud Spiritually-Blinded People on the Earth. However, there is Hope for Europeans, Mexicans, Chinese, Russians, Indians, Malaysians, Indonesians, Filipinos, Africans, Australians, South Americans, Central Americans, and American Indians, who are Humble and Honest enough to Confess that Americans are some of the most Stupid People who ever Lived, most of whom are Unworthy to Live in those **"Beautiful Swanky PALACES"**: beCause of Mocking your Inspired Books, if nothing else. {See www.Amazon.com for: **"Are Americans the Most STUPID People who ever Lived?" (HOW Working People can PROSPER and Live in PEACE Under the Rulership of a RIGHTEOUS KING!) By The Worldwide People's Revolution!®** Book 047.}

— Chapter 14 —

The Birth of a New Nation!

14-01 [_] Now, under Ideal Circumstances, the Intellectual Educated People in this World of Wonders will soon come to Discover my Inspired Books, and fall in Love with them: beCause of the many Good Reasons and Great Advantages for Building Beautiful Planned City States. {See **"The Right Design for Living!" (A List of Great Advantages of Building Beautiful Planned City States!) By The Worldwide People's Revolution!®** Book 012, which is a Companion Book of: **"The Low Court of Supreme Injustices is Brought to Trial!" (The Worldwide People's Revolution!® Butts Heads with the United States Supreme Court, with or without their Black Robes of Hypocrisies and Lies!)**, Book 011, which is a Companion Book of: **"Poverty Hunger Riots Strikes Brutalities Election Deceptions and Civil Wars!" (The High Price that we Earthlings have Paid for Leaving the Good Land!)** Book 014.} And then those People will Act WISELY, and Increase their Bank Accounts by Selling my Inspired Books, which will not only make them Happier and thus Healthier; but, it will also Increase the Happiness and Good Health of whomever Buys and Reads all such Books, which will Greatly Increase the Faith, Hope, Trust, Love, Patience, Persistence, and Obedience of Mankind in general, who will eventually "See the Light," and get Inspired to Establish a NEW Nation in America, with a New Constitution. {See www.Amazon.com for: **"The CONSTITUTION for the New RIGHTEOUS One-World GovernMINT!" (HOW all Peoples can get True Justice, and Celebrate the Great Year of JUBILEE!) By The Worldwide People's Revolution!®**, Book 016, which will Naturally Inspire them to Build **"The Great World TEMPLE of PEACE!" (The Glory of Jerusalem Arises Again!)**, Book 017, which could be Built in **"The United States of the Whole World!" (A True Global Economy for the Masses of Working People!) By The Worldwide People's Revolution!®** Book 055.}

14-02 [_] O Elected King, would the Israelis not ENVY us Americans, if we Built the Great World Temple of Peace in this Country, instead of in Jerusalem, which will be the Headquarters for **"The New RIGHTEOUS One-World Government!"**?

14-03 [_] Well, Envy or not, it is Possible that Americans will DEMAND it. After all, there is Plenty of Space in the Great State of Flexible Texas for a City that is 8+ Miles in diameter and nearly a Mile Tall.

14-04 [_] O Elected King, it seems that most Americans would not be Interested in Trashing their Long-enduring Constitution, in Favor of your Constitution, which is not even Completed. †§‡

14-05 [_] Well, actually, they will be able to Keep their Old Constitution, as well as their False Federal Government: beCause the New RIGHTEOUS One-World Government will be a Separate Government System, altogether, whereby those **"GLORIOUS Swanky Hotels Castles and Fortresses"** will be Independent of all Nations, and will only Trade and Deal with other Swanky Fortresses, by Means of Underground Electric Trains, until at last they Overtake all of the Nations, and Grow like a Great Mountain, just as *the Book of Daniel* Prophesies. (See Chapter 2:40—45, KJV.)

14-06 [_] O Elected King, if it is the Will of God, we cannot Change it: beCause, whatever is supposed to be, will be. (See Daniel 11:36, KJV.)

14-07 [_] Well, that certainly follows the Doctrine of Predestination, which has yet to be Proven in a Courtroom. ‡

14-08 [_] O Elected King, I do not care to get myself Entangled in the Mysterious Words of the Unholy Mutilated Bible; but, after Listening to Retired General John Allen at the Democratic National Convention, in July of 2016, I am Fully Persuaded that the Divided States of United Lies are DOOMED: beCause of their PRIDE, which comes before Destruction. (See Proverbs 16:18.)

14-09 [_] Well, I must Confess that it was not a very Humble Speech, which can be found on C-SPAN, about 5 Hours into the Convention on Thursday, July 28th, 2016. Indeed, "the greatest nation in the world" is likely to be Reduced to Radioactive Ashes, if Americans do not Humble themselves by Means of Fasting and Praying, and Confess ALL of their Sins, and Change their Ways of Thinking and Living, and Build those **"GLORIOUS Swanky Hotels Castles and Fortresses!"** Yes, the Muslims can Build their Cities, and the Christians can Build their Cities, and the Black People can Build their Cities, and the Mexicans can Build their Cities, and each Group of Religious or Non-religious People can Build their Cities, and all can Live in Peace with True Prosperity.

14-10 [_] O Elected King, may God Hasten that Glad Day.

(The so-called "United States of North America," in Disguise!)

— Chapter 15 —

The Conclusion

15-01 [_] Now, whether or not you Agree or Disagree with what I Propose to do is of no Concern to God, who will Judge you According to your Words and WORKS. (See *Matthew 12:37,* and *the Book of Revelation 20:12, KJV.*) Therefore, if you Say that you Love God; but, do not Care for his Good Earth, and do your Part to Help Destroy it, you will be Judged for it, even as I will also be Judged for it. However, as of now, we are Forced to be Hypocrites: beCause we are Caught in Satan's Trap, who would not even know HOW to Live without those Stinking Noisy Polluting Vehicles: because our Lifestyles are Arranged According to Satan's Plan, and not God's Plan. Therefore, until we Build those **"GLORIOUS Swanky Hotels Castles and Fortresses,"** we will not be Able to Escape from the Capitalist Trap, and be set Free with a Capital F, whereby we will be Free in Deed. Otherwise, the Parades to Hell will go on, and Humanity will Suffer with what is known as *"the Great Tribulation." — Matthew 24.*

15-02 [_] Oh you Silly Ignorant king, I would not Fear to put the Baby Jesus into a Stroller, and walk directly behind anyone of those so-called Stinking Noisy Vehicles, where he could Breathe the Exhaust directly from the Tailpipe, just to Prove to you that God would not Object to our Use of Diesel Fuel, even if that Exhaust is as Black as Soot: because, it is not that which Enters into a Person's Nostrils that Defiles him; but, it is that which comes Out of his Mouth, such as your Unholy Words of Satanic Blasphemy! †§‡§§

15-03 [_] Well, you cannot be Serious. The Baby Jesus would Strongly Object to such Mistreatments, even to be taken onto such Polluted Highways, and especially in Poor Countries, where the Vehicles are not very well Tuned Up, which Spew Out Black Toxic Capitalist Poisons, which Truths all People should have to Confess, or else have their Noses held up to such Tailpipes, while the Vehicles are running, whereby they might Discover how BAD those Vehicles are.

15-04 [_] O Elected King, that Person should Apologize to God for Seeking to Justify all such Abominations as those Cars, Motorcycles, Motor Scooters, Lawnmowers, Garden Tillers, Weed-eaters, Chainsaws, Snow Blowers, Snowmobiles, Vans, Pickups, Trucks, Buses, Tractors, Backhoes, Bulldozers, and especially Airplanes, which are the Worst of Polluters, just after those Coal-powered ElecTrickery Plants, which should all be Shut Down: because they are filling the Sky with Mercury, Lead, Arsenic, Cadmium, and God knows what else! †‡

15-05 [_] O Elected King, if God did not Want us to Use all such Black Greasy Oily Substances, WHY did he Create them?

15-06 [_] He wanted to Discover the Honest Righteous People, who will DEMAND **"The Great Worldwide TELEVISED Court HEARING,"** whereby it can be Proven to be Good or Evil.

15-07 [_] Okay, I give up! HOW should we go about DEMANDING that Great Meeting of the Most Intelligent Minds?

15-08 [_] Well, first of all, we must Multiply these Books, and all of the Inspired Books that are Listed in Chapter 16, which everyone Needs to Study, just to get their Thinking Straightened Out.

15-09 [_] I could never Manage to Read all such Books during one Lifetime, let alone before the Arctic Ice is Totally MELTED.

15-10 [_] Well, just Read as much as you can, and Hope to God that you Escape from the Great Tribulation: because it will not be any Fun. {See www.Amazon.com for: **"The Secret City of the Great King!" (HOW the True Church will Escape from the Great Tribulation!) By The Worldwide People's Revolution!®** Book 042.

(The so-called "United States of North America," in Disguise!)

— Chapter 16 —

A "Long Boring List" of other Fascinating Books by the same Inspired Author!

16-001 [_] **"LIGHTNING Versus the Lightning Bug!" (HOW almost Everyone can become Moderately RICH, without Telling Any Lies nor Selling Any Trash!) By The Worldwide People's Revolution!®** Book 001. The Cover Photo shows a Beautiful Sunrise in the Blest Land of Eternal Springtime!

16-002 [_] **"What is WRong with those Professing Christians?" (A Self-Examination of the Heart of the Body of Good Government!) By The Worldwide People's Revolution!®** Book 002. The Cover Photo shows a Small Portion of our Unfinished Retirement Home.

16-003 [_] **"For the Love of Money!" (The Strange Things that People Say and Do to Get more Money!) By The Worldwide People's Revolution!®** Book 003. The Cover Photo shows a Jewish Boy studying the *Scriptures*.

16-004 [_] **"HOW to Prepare for CLIMATE CHANGES!" (The Wisest Plan for Mankind to Follow!) By The Worldwide People's Revolution!®** Book 004. The Cover Photo shows Dark Awesome Clouds.

16-005 [_] **"WHY do I have to be Surrounded by CRAZY PEOPLE?" (Do almost all People Feel like they are Surrounded by CRAZY PEOPLE??) By The Worldwide People's Revolution!®** Book 005. The Cover Photo shows Delicious Fragrant Ripe Mangos.

16-006 [_] **"The Washington Journal is a FARCE!" (C-SPAN Managers are not very WISE!) By The Worldwide People's Revolution!®** Book 006. The Cover Photo shows a Portion of "Mars," up close.

16-007 [_] **"The PRAYERS of PUMPKINHEADS!" (Even God Needs a Little Humor to Cheer himself Up!) By The Worldwide People's Revolution!®** Book 007. The Cover Photo shows the Author's Brother standing beside a very large Tree in the Blest Land of Eternal Springtime.

16-008 [_] **"A Sound Argument for Masters and Servants!" (WHY Everyone Needs a Good Master, and every Master Needs Good Obedient Servants!) By The Worldwide People's Revolution!®** Book 008. The Cover Photo shows a Pleasant Manmade Waterfalls.

16-009 [_] **"WHY are some Preachers so POOR?" (HOW almost all Preachers could Get RICH, without Preaching any Outlandish LIES!) By The Worldwide People's Revolution!®** Book 009. The Cover Photo shows a Portion of the Inside of a Gold-laden Church in the Blest Land of Eternal Springtime, worth a Billion Dollars!

16-010 [_] **"GOOD NEWS for REBEL WOMEN!"** (HOW almost all Wives can become Moderately Rich without Leaving their Homes! Guaranteed!) By The Worldwide People's Revolution!® Book 010. The Cover Photo shows Beautiful Ceramic Work in the Blest Land of Eternal Springtime.

16-011 [_] **"The Low Court of Supreme Injustices is Brought to Trial!"** (The Worldwide People's Revolution Butts Heads with the United States Supreme Court, with or without their Black Robes of Hypocrisies and Lies!) By The Worldwide People's Revolution!® Book 011. The Cover Photo shows the United States Supreme Court Building in Washington.

16-012 [_] **"The Right Design for Living!"** (A List of Great Advantages for Building Beautiful Planned City States!) By The Worldwide People's Revolution!® Book 012. The Cover Photo shows the Great Pyramid at Chichen Itza, in Mexico.

16-013 [_] **"The Gospel According to The Worldwide People's Revolution!"** (The Good News from the Most Modern Perspective!) By The Worldwide People's Revolution!® Book 013. The Cover Photo shows a very Dirty Drunkard lying by the Street in the Cursed Land of Childish Rebellion, which does not Believe in Righteous Kings.

16-014 [_] **"Poverty Hunger Riots Strikes Brutalities Election Deceptions and Civil Wars!"** (The High Price that we Earthlings have Paid for Leaving the Good Land!) By The Worldwide People's Revolution!® Book 014. The Cover Photo shows Tombs in a Cemetery.

16-015 [_] **"Seven Great Armies of Working Soldiers!"** (HOW to Provide a Way for Everyone to WORK: so as to Eliminate Poverty, Crimes, Drug Abuses, Prisons and Unnecessary Taxes!) By The Worldwide People's Revolution!® Book 015. The Cover Photo shows a Truckload of Potential Working Soldiers.

16-016 [_] **"The CONSTITUTION for the New RIGHTEOUS One-World GovernMint!"** (HOW all Peoples can get True Justice, and Celebrate the Great Year of JUBILEE!) By The Worldwide People's Revolution!® Book 016. The Cover Photo shows a Gathering Thunderstorm.

16-017 [_] **"The Great World TEMPLE of PEACE!"** (The Glory of Jerusalem Arises Again!) By The Worldwide People's Revolution!® Book 017. The Cover Photo shows Old Jerusalem in all of its Naked and Potential Glory.

16-018 [_] **"The Swanky Associations of Working Soldiers!"** (A Fascinating Collection of Various Kinds of Voluntary Working Soldiers!) By The Worldwide People's Revolution!® Book 018. The Cover Photo shows a Beautiful Malachite Pyramid.

16-019 [_] **"GLORIOUS Swanky Hotels Castles and Fortresses!"** (Beautiful Planned City States for WISE Intelligent Well-Educated People with Common Sense and Good Understanding!) By The Worldwide People's Revolution!® Book 019. The Cover Photo shows a Beautiful "Million-dollar" Onyx Box in all of its Naked Glory.

(The so-called "United States of North America," in Disguise!)

16-020 [_] **"Are you a Jobless Graduate of the SKQL uv FQLZ?" (HOW to Get a GOUD EJUKAASHUN without Robbing the Bank!) By The Worldwide People's Revolution!®** Book 020. The Cover Photo shows a small and Beautiful Onyx Vase.

16-021 [_] **"The LUSCIOUS All-Mineral Organic Method of Gardening!" (HOW to Grow DELICIOUS Satisfying Foods for Potential Kingz and Kweenz in Swanky PALACES!) By The Worldwide People's Revolution!®** Book 021. The Cover Photo shows Beautiful Green Terraces in the Blest Land of Eternal Summertime.

16-022 [_] **"Did God or Satan Ordain Medical Doctors??" (Ask Huck Finn and/or Nigger Jim: because neither Tom Sawyer nor Judge Thatcher would Know!) By The Worldwide People's Revolution!®** Book 022. The Cover Photo shows Pretty Flowers at a Tomb.

16-023 [_] **"The BIG White OUTHOUSE on the Not-so-Biblical Capitol DUNGHILL!" (The Chief Sins of the Divided States of United Lies!) By The Worldwide People's Revolution!®** Book 023. The Cover Photo shows the Capitol Building in Washington, District of Criminals, District of Confusion, District of Colombian Drug Addicts, etc., etc.

16-024 [_] **"The Public School of IGNERUNT FQLZ!" (HOW we have been GRAATLEE DISEEVD!) By The Worldwide People's Revolution!®** Book 024. The Cover Photo shows a Disorganized Fruit Market in a City of Confusion.

16-025 [_] **"In thu Beeginingz uv Thingz!" (Thu Kreeaashun Stooree frum thu Beegining!) By The Worldwide People's Revolution!®** Book 025. The Cover Photo shows a Yellow Sapote, which not one Person in a Million has ever Tasted, in spite of being one of the most Pleasant Sweetest Fruits known to Mankind, which does not Ship very well, which must Ripen on the Tree, in order to be Extremely GOOD, as in "Heavenly Good!"

16-026 [_] **"God Speaks and the Whole World Listens!" (Fire on the Mountain from the Burning Bush by the Spirit of Truth!) By The Worldwide People's Revolution!®** Book 026. The Cover Photo shows the Sign or Flag for **"The New RIGHTEOUS One-World Government!"**

16-027 [_] **"Does a Good Soldier have to be a MURDERER?" (Seven Great Swanky Armies of Voluntary Working Soldiers!) By The Worldwide People's Revolution!®** Book 027. Dan.

16-028 [_] **"Thu Nq MAGNUFIID Verzhun uv Thu PROVERBZ uv KING SOLUMUN in Plaan Ingglish!" (The Understandable Version of the Famous Proverbs of King Solomon in Plain English!) By The Worldwide People's Revolution!®** Book 028. The Cover Photo shows Gemstones in an Onyx Jewelry Box.

16-029 [_] **"UNLIMITED ENERJEE 99 Percent Pollutions Free!" (HOW to Obtain FREE ElecTrickery, Worldwide!) By The Worldwide People's Revolution!®** Book 029. The Cover Photo shows an Onyx Tray for a large Spoon in the Kitchen.

16-030 [_] **"FREEDUM uv SPEECH!" (U Speshoul Maguzeen uv Onust Upinyunz!) By The Worldwide People's Revolution!®** Book 030-0001. The Cover Photo shows a Portion of

47

one of the Author's Marble Countertops, worth 100$ per square foot, for an Example of what you could also have, if you Exercise your Faith, Hope, Trust, Love, Patience, Persistence, and OBEDIENCE!

16-031 [_] "A Sure Cure for GUN VIOLENCE!" (HOW TO STOP GANG WARS and CRIMINAL SHOOTINGS!) By The Worldwide People's Revolution!® Book 031. The Cover Photo shows a Short Shotgun, which is fully loaded and ready for any Tax Master who might Attempt to Steel the Retirement Home, who never moved a Finger to Help Build it, whose Anti-Christ False Federal Cover-up WICKED Government allowed Banksters to Rob us of 30 Years of Hard Work and 300,000+ dollars-worth of Investments in our Uncommon American Farm. (Future Books will have Cover Photos of some of that Hard Work. Please be Patient.)

16-032 [_] "AIIRMWVC and Reasonable Solutions!" (Aliens, Illegal Immigrants, Refugees, Migrant Workers and other Victims of Capitalism!) By The Worldwide People's Revolution!® Book 032. The Cover Photo shows a "Sea of People."

16-033 [_] "Mark Twain Races for the PRESIDENCY!" (The 2016 Presidential Candidates Desperately Need Some STRONG Undefeatable COMPETITION!) By The Worldwide People's Revolution!® Book 033. The Cover Photo shows a Mountain Goat and a Silver Dollar.

16-034 [_] "ECCLESIASTES UNCOVERED!" (The New MAGNIFIED Version of Ecclesiastes and the Song of Solomon in Plain English!) By The Worldwide People's Revolution!® Book 034. The Cover Photo shows a Peacock Resting.

16-035 [_] "The Environmentalists' Paradise!" (HOW almost Everyone could be Living in a Beautiful Manmade Paradise!) By The Worldwide People's Revolution!® Book 035. The Cover Photo shows an Artist's Conception of Paradise for a single Family in the Blest Land of Perfect Oneness, where all is at Peace.

16-036 [_] "The Seven Basic Spiritual Building Blocks of LIFE!" (Faith Hope Trust Love Patience Persistence and Obedience!) By The Worldwide People's Revolution!® Book 036. The Cover Photo shows Onion Domes trimmed with Gold.

16-037 [_] "DIETS!" (A Reasonable Solution for the "Eternal Controversy"!) By The Worldwide People's Revolution!® Book 037. The Cover Photo shows some Colorful Fruits.

16-038 [_] "The Nature of CAPITALISM!" (A List of the EVILS of CAPITALISM!) By The Worldwide People's Revolution!® Book 038. The Cover Photo shows a Pretty Red Car.

16-039 [_] "SWANGKEENOMIKS Rules the Roost!" (HOW all People can Prosper in a RIIT WAA, and STOP Polluting the Earth with Capitalist TRASH!) By The Worldwide People's Revolution!® Book 039. The Cover Photo shows a small Portion of our Retirement Home before the 5,000+ square-foot Roof was Installed.

16-040 [_] "The New MAGNIFIED Version of The Book of MOORMUN!" (The Story of the White and Dark Indians in the Americas!) By The Worldwide People's Revolution!® Book 040, Volumes 1 and 2. The Cover Photos show the Queen of England's Golden Coach, and one of our Marbleous Spanish Walls, which is worth a thousand dollars per square Yard, installed on 7 similar Walls, which are 12 feet long. It is very Inspiring. No one could Study it for very long without Believing in a Great Creator God.

16-041 [_] "The Great Worldwide TELEVISED Court HEARING!" (That Great Meeting of the Most Intelligent Minds!) By The Worldwide People's Revolution!® Book 041. The Cover Photo shows Mount Popotits covered with Snow.

16-042 [_] "The Secret City of the Great King!" (HOW the True Church will Escape from the Great Tribulation!) By The Worldwide People's Revolution!® Book 042. The Cover Photo shows a Colorful Ferris Wheel. P-5877.

16-043 [_] "Terrorists Beware that your Days are Numbered!" (HOW to Bring those Terrorist Attacks to a Screeching HALT!) By The Worldwide People's Revolution!® Book 043. The Cover Photo shows a Picture of George Warmonger Bush. This Book also contains the Fascinating Book of LEHI.

16-044 [_] "The New MAGNIFIED Version of ISAIAH in Plain English!" (The Understandable Version of the Book of Isaiah!) By The Worldwide People's Revolution!® Book 044. The Cover Photo shows a Swanky Potato / Avocado Salad with Sweet Peas and Corn.

16-045 [_] "HOW to Become a HOLY Man!" (40 Good Reasons WHY People Should FAST and PRAY!) By The Worldwide People's Revolution!® Book 045. The Cover Photo will show a Holy Man, just as soon as one Presents himself for the Photograph.

16-046 [_] "The Proper RULES for FASTING!" (The Complete Instruction Manual for True Repentance!) By The Worldwide People's Revolution!® Book 046. The Cover Photo shows an Unclean Man.

16-047 [_] "Are Americans the Most STUPID People who ever Lived?" (HOW Working People can PROSPER and Live in PEACE Under the Rulership of a RIGHTEOUS KING!) By The Worldwide People's Revolution!® Book 047. The Cover Photo shows a large Portion of the Author's Marbleous Living Room Floor, which is worth 100,000$.

16-048 [_] "An Amazing Collection of Wit and Wisdom!" (The Marvelous Tale of the Colorful Peacock from Angel Ridge, and the Strong Rope of Hope!) By The Worldwide People's Revolution!® Book 048. The Cover Photo shows a Book Display.

16-049 [_] "Justifications for Capitalizations!" (WHY The Worldwide People's Revolution!® Defies the School of Fools by Capitalizing Love and Hate!) By The Worldwide People's Revolution!® Book 049. The Cover Photo shows a Water Tower.

16-050 [_] "The END of CONFUSION!" (The Great CELEBRATION of the Magnificent Wedding of the Humble Honest Nations, and the Grand Year of JUBILEE!) By The Worldwide People's Revolution!® Book 050. The Cover Photo shows a Portion of a Colorful Parade.

16-051 [_] "**The Loathsome Burdens of the Independent Jackasses!**" (A New Approach for Solving our Massive Problems!) **By The Worldwide People's Revolution!**® Book 051. The Cover Photo shows a Spanish Military Barracks.

16-052 [_] "**Are we Tax Slaves of a Lower Order than Lying Red JEWS?**" (HOW to be Liberated from all Slavery, Worldwide!) **By The Worldwide People's Revolution!**® Book 052. The Cover Photo shows a few Tax Slaves.

16-053 [_] "**The Great False Economy is now DEBUNKED!**" (Adolf Hitler had a much Better Economic System!) **By The Worldwide People's Revolution!**® Book 053. The Cover Photo shows a Capitalist Toilet Brush.

16-054 [_] "**The UGLY Scarred Dishonest Face of Poor Old Miserable UNCLE SAM!**" (A Memorial Day Legacy!) **By The Worldwide People's Revolution!**® Book 054. The Cover Photo shows a Poster of "Uncle Sam," who Symbolizes the Federal Government of **"The Divided States of United Lies!"**

16-055 [_] "**The United States of the Whole World!**" (A True Global Economy for the Masses of Working People!) **By The Worldwide People's Revolution!**® Book 055. A Photo of a 110-year-old Well-made Mexican Rocking Chair with a Cowhide Seat.

16-056 [_] "**The New RIGHTEOUS One-World Government!**" (HOW to Establish a Righteous One-World Government without Going to WAR!) **By The Worldwide People's Revolution!**® Book 056. The Cover Photo shows the Flag of that Good Government.

16-057 [_] "**Those Ridiculous Contradictions within the Holy Bible!**" (HOW to Read the Bible with an Open Mind!) **By The Worldwide People's Revolution!**® Book 057. The Cover Photo shows a Purple Tree.

16-058 [_] "**The Divided States of United Lies!**" (The so-called "United States of North America," in Disguise!) **By The Worldwide People's Revolution!**® Book 058. The Cover Photo shows a Map of the United States.

16-059 [_] "**The Complete SURVEYS of our VALUES!**" (SURVEYS of Religious Spiritual Political Governmental Sexual Social Moral Economic Business Labor Habitual and Miscellaneous VALUES! **By The Worldwide People's Revolution!**® Book 059. The Cover Photo shows a Large Onyx Vase in the Author's Palace.

16-060 [_] "**HOW to Get our PRIORITIES in ORDER!**" (The Glories of Democracy; and, Does DEMON-ocracy have its Priorities in Order?) **By The Worldwide People's Revolution!**® Book 060. The Cover Photo shows a Different View of that Large Onyx Vase.

16-061 [_] "**The New MAGNIFIED Version of the GOOD NEWS According to Saint LUKE!**" (The Magnified Gospel of Luke in Plain English!) **By The Worldwide People's Revolution!**® Book 061. The Cover Photo shows Agate Windows.

(The so-called "United States of North America," in Disguise!)

16-062 [_] **"The New MAGNIFIED Version of the GOOD NEWS According to Saint JOHN!"** (The Gospel According to Saint John Zebedee Boanerges in Plain English!) **By The Worldwide People's Revolution!®** Book 062. The Cover Photo shows the Parthenon.

16-063 [_] **"The New MAGNIFIED Version of the Book of ACTS!"** (The Understandable Version of the ACTS of the Apostles in Plain English!) By The Worldwide People's Revolution!® Book 063. The Cover Photo shows a Small Portion of Arches National Park.

16-064 [_] **"The New MAGNIFIED Version of the PSALMS of King David!"** (The Understandable Version of the Famous Psalms in Plain English!) By The Worldwide People's Revolution!® Book 064. The Cover Photo shows some of the Grand Canyon.

16-065 [_] **"A List of FAIR Swanky Wages!"** (The Equitable Wage System!) By The Worldwide People's Revolution!® Book 065. The Cover Photo shows a Pile of Money.

16-066 [_] **"Beautiful Swanky PALACES!"** (A New Concept in Living Habits!) By The Worldwide People's Revolution!® Book 066. The Cover Photo shows a Bouquet of Pretty Flowers. P-6136.

16-067 [_] **"The Swanky Sword of Divine Truths!"** (The Most Powerful Weapon in the Whole Universe!) By The Worldwide People's Revolution!® Book 067. The Cover Photo shows a Sword.

{NOTE: This List of Available Books will be Updated Periodically. If you fail to find any of these Books on Amazon.com, just be Patient: because I am a One-Man Army, you might say. All of the Books are written, and just need to be Posted, after they are Updated.}

The Divided States of United Lies has just about come to the End of its Rope of Hopelessness: beCause of the Rejection of Provable Truths without any Justifiable Reasons, which is a Major Sin in the Eyes of God, who Loves all that is GOOD, which does not Include any Capitalist Abominations, which People can Live Happily without, even as Jesus Christ and his Disciples Lived without such Evil Things. However, you might not even Believe in Jesus Christ: beCause of False Christians, who are Poor Representatives of him, which would Include most of the Politicians, Doctors, Lawyers, Judges, News Reporters and Preachers, themselves, who have Completely Missed the Mark, you might say, while Aiming at the Moon. Whatever the Case, it is now Time to Face the Facts, and get our House in Order, before we find ourselves in the middle of an Evil Thing called the Great Tribulation!

www.ingramcontent.com/pod-product-compliance
Lightning Source LLC
Chambersburg PA
CBHW080559190526
45169CB00007B/2820